"I have had the privilege of watching Larry Anderson 'live' many of the experiences which form the foundation for this book. I'm delighted that he has chosen to share with others the main concepts leading to his professional growth and personal development."

STEPHEN C. PERRY
President
Toledo Scale Corporation

"I have profited from reading Working for Success. *It presents, in an easy-to-read form, success principles that work!"*

DENNIS H. SHREVE
Engineering Manager
IRD Mechanalysis, Inc.

"Larry Anderson has taken a complex and timely subject and made it possible to understand and use his success principles daily."

JOHN J. GARY, Ph.D.
Professional Trainer/Counselor
Worthington, Ohio

WORKING FOR SUCCESS

BY

Larry Anderson

Published by
Anderson & Anderson, Inc.
P.O. Box 26416
Columbus, Ohio   43226

Library of Congress
Catalog Card Number: 88–70593
ISBN   0–9620270–0–6

Printed in the United States of America

Dedicated to

*My business associates whose help and ideas
have enabled us to be successful together;*

*My wife, Carol, who has supported me through
all the trials and successes of my career;*

and to

*Our children, Eric, Todd, and Jennifer.
This book is my gift to commemorate their
growing up and working at their life plans.*

My Own Story

My career drifted along for many years without any definite plan or objective. I felt that I was making some progress when compared to those around me, and appearances would indicate that I was successful, considering my overall standard of living. However, no matter how hard I worked, I did not feel satisfied or in control. Job conditions appeared to go from challenging opportunities to dismal disappointments. I changed jobs several times in hopes of gaining more experience and a better feeling of success. But my attitude about job conditions soon acquired the familiar sense of disappointment. Instead of feeling successful, I felt unhappy.

Over the years, I read about or knew personally a few people who achieved major success either locally or nationally. I could not understand how some people could have enormous success while I was struggling along. How is it possible for an actor to be President of the United States? How can a thirty-four-year-old Englishman build a profitable trans-Atlantic airline company? After being fired from his first job, how did an engineer build a premier aircraft manufacturing corporation? "Luck" was the easy answer to my questions about the successes of other people, my hit-and-miss successes, and my destiny.

So, as I hoped for my "luck" to come through, I plodded on. Although confused and unhappy, I was learning a great deal about the technical side of my profession. I also developed an appreciation for some equally important "people skills." I realized that having the ability to work with and through people is a very desirable trait. Even as my technical and people skills grew, however, I did not understand the *true* cause of my successes or failures. I was not *consciously* aware of laws or success principles at work. In fact, I was making progress with my career by using some important principles having to do with the use of mental powers — but using them quite unconsciously.

The problem of understanding the real source of success bothered me for a long time. Then, after several years of small successes, study, and observation, I finally realized the TRUTH about success principles. The truth is this: *Natural laws of human endeavor are set into motion by my mental powers* and, therefore, *I can control the outcome* in the form of accomplishments leading to recognition, compensation, and growth. Furthermore, I can create the work environment that brings enjoyment, success, and, eventually, happiness that flows into other parts of my life. The true source of success is no longer a mystery.

I have used this new knowledge in a practical manner to take control of my job, my career, and my destiny. With some effort on my part, I have developed a career plan that is appropriate for me. I do work that is enjoyable, and achieve a feeling of satisfaction and success every day. Finally, I have a clear picture of where I am going. How marvelous my life is now! This exuberance for work and life became possible for me because I began to use the success principles fully to change my distorted beliefs and increase my mental capacity, and because I now realize that *successful people use their mental powers consciously.* Concentrating on the conscious use of my full mental capacity made a difference in my life.

Using lessons learned over the years, I have prepared the "Working for Success" Plan. Those readers who choose to use the Plan will (1) discover a personal plan for success; (2) create the kind of job conditions that are satisfying; (3) achieve performance levels that will be rewarded by employers. They will gain self-confidence as the Plan enables them to have the understanding that comes both from knowing how employers think and from working in accord with the natural laws dealing with human endeavors.

The Plan has helped many of my associates to take control of their jobs and career development. They have become more productive on the job and have a greater sense of accomplishment. It is now my desire to share the "Working for Success" Plan with America's work force. Each employee can benefit by acquiring enjoyable job conditions, achieving career success, and gaining personal happiness, and, concurrently, by con-

tributing to his/her employer's business success.
There is no doubt in my mind that if we would all
use the success principles of the Plan consciously,
American business could win the competitive bat-
tle in the international market place. Together, we
can work to eliminate the current productivity
deficit and return America to its rightful world
leadership role.

Author

Contents

Get Started Now

Many employees think of their offices as prisons where, for forty hours each week, they "do time." Frustrations and disappointments are frequent. They are sure that, for one reason or another, things will never change. Some feel they are too old to be found desirable by company management or by another employer. Many experienced employees believe that their lack of a college education is the reason that advancement within their company is impossible. New employees starting out at the bottom may feel hopelessness because they lack the experience necessary for a better job.

On the contrary, *anyone* can achieve career success — under any conditions and at any age. There are notable examples of people who made significant changes in their careers, which led them to success. America's first billionaire was a small-time mechanic until he was in his forties: his name was Henry Ford. Ray Kroc, the creator of the McDonald's food chain, was an average salesman until he was in his fifties. Kentucky Fried Chicken restaurants originated when Colonel Sanders was in his sixties, and President Reagan was in his seventies when he was first sworn in as President of the United States! Young people can be great successes, too. The creator of the popular Cabbage Patch Kids dolls and the creators of highly successful Apple Computers were only in their twenties when they started their companies.

While these examples have received national publicity, there are millions of success stories that don't reach the news media. It is not necessary to start up a new business to be successful as an individual. One can have a successful career experience within a corporation, whatever one's job conditions may be at the present time. Look around where you work, and see if you recognize individuals who are achievers — who are confident, in control, and happy. It is likely these successful individuals didn't always enjoy success. However, since they are now recognized by management as valuable employees, these achievers are likely to receive top financial compensation and opportunities for career development.

It isn't always easy to predict which individuals will become these high achievers. For instance, physical appearance won't give you a clue as to why some people rise from mediocrity to celebrity. The way a person looks may add or detract from ultimate success, but the most important source for success is located within the individual. In every case, there are unseen causes which have their roots in the mental realm. It is *mental capacity* that determines the success of the individual.

You may acknowledge the importance of one's mental capacity to one's success, yet you may still be experiencing frustrations and disappointments instead of success. This is because even though you may "know" something about a subject, you don't always "experience" it. For example, when I was a small child, my teacher taught me to spell my own name. At first, I knew it could be done, I saw how it was done, yet I was not quite able to accomplish the task. I tried spelling my name several times, but I was only able to complete my name with great effort and complete concentration. As time went by, I became able to spell my name without thinking about it. The ability to spell my name had entered my consciousness — knowledge transformed into a skill. In business, you may "know" some facts about success, yet you haven't achieved the success you would like. You may not have committed yourself to concentrating upon success principles until they have become new skills.

In the same manner, you do not wholly accept information until you do so consciously. Facts or statements presented to you will not help you unless you intentionally choose to accept the information as true. My wife was asked to sell advertising space in our high school football program as a means of raising funds for a parents' support group. At first, she felt uncomfortable accepting the assignment of contacting local merchants to solicit their orders. Several of her friends and I told her that she had all the necessary abilities to do the job. After some deliberation, she decided to try, and started to make the calls. Within three days, she sold all the space allocated to her, because she accepted our encouragement, made the contacts, and found merchants receptive to the opportunity. Now, my wife knows she can sell. This information is part of her consciousness. Information about yourself or the potential you represent will have no value for you unless you choose to acknowledge facts about the real YOU.

The real YOU is the consciousness you experience. Words like awareness, knowledge, recognition, feeling, intelligence, understanding, sense, mind, and thought relate to the consciousness of an individual. Within your consciousness, your value system and belief system combine to produce your character and personality. Your consciousness can continue in its present state, or you can choose to develop it (and thereby develop your *self*) by using your ability to think — your mental capacity.

Study, concentrate, practice, and think about the truth presented in *Working for Success* until it becomes part of your consciousness. You *can* turn success principles into mental skills, and you *can* use factual information to accomplish your career goals. Start now by reading this book all the way through while reflecting on your circum-

GET STARTED NOW   11

stances. If you choose to accept the information presented, you can discover your mental potential and arouse your success resources. You must make a commitment to yourself to use the success principles for at least three months if you want proof that you possess real success power. Then, for lifelong success, you will be excited to continue the commitment to work every day to achieve your success.

Please start now, and stick with it. You have everything to gain!

Introduction

University studies have revealed that on a daily basis approximately eighty percent of America's work force goes to work reluctantly. Haven't you seen associates who are unwilling to be cooperative, or slow to get their work done, or resentful when assigned a project, or unenthusiastic about good news? In most cases, aren't these the same people who look highly motivated at quitting time? Are these people the same employees who do only average work? No wonder our country's product quality and customer service performance have become second-rate!

How do *you* feel about going to work? Are you part of that reluctant eighty percent? Could it be that your job conditions at work are not pleasing or satisfying? Maybe you are experiencing some of the following negative job conditions:

* emotional stress and pressure to perform,
* worry about survival and security,
* misunderstandings with the boss,
* poor pay, hours, and employee benefits,
* poor opportunity to learn or be trained,
* interruptions and changes in priorities,
* errors by others that affect you,
* unreasonable tasks and assignments,
* criticism and gossip about you,
* good deeds being ignored,

* uncomfortable work area,
* lack of challenge and direction,
* favoritism,
* and more . . .

What do you face when you get to work? The office, the desk, the left-over business from the day before, the first telephone call, and THE FIRST PROBLEM! As the day goes on, does it appear evident that you do not control events and circumstances affecting you? Do you find yourself doing the things that other people want to have done instead of what you want to do?

How about your progress in developing a satisfying career, when each day has such tough challenges and problems? You work hard at the job each day, but will this effort lead you to the career success you wish for? Are you happy, do you have a sense of accomplishment, are you fulfilled? Who can make sure you find enjoyable job conditions, career success, and personal happiness?

Experience has taught us to blame our problems and shortcomings on our companies, our superiors, or our work associates. We have been trained to depend on others. As small children, we looked to our mothers and fathers. Our parents provided us with everything. As wage earners, we look to our employers as means of support. Rarely do we look within for the answers to our questions and problems.

Thus, the enormous intellectual power of the subconscious mind lies idle because we are not aware that we can use its vast resources. We use approximately ten percent of our mental resources, and this ten percent, influenced by our basic five senses, manages our thinking. We are certainly successful with our senses of taste, touch, sight, smell, and hearing. But how successful are we with our "inner sense" when we examine the incredible power of our subconscious mind? Ninety percent of our mental abilities lies dormant even though we have the power within ourselves to awaken these resources — the power to reach our potential!

What is your potential? How do you know what your potential is, and what can you do to demonstrate your abilities? What can you do to achieve success at your job and career? How can you attract better job conditions and career opportunities? What is necessary to earn better pay and benefits? Where should you be in the business world to contribute to humanity and gain a feeling of satisfaction and success?

Working for Success will help you answer these questions and more. The book you now hold will enable you to get from where you are today to where you wish to be in the future. Written in a manner easy to understand and put into practice, *Working for Success* is divided into three sections: Section I — "*BE* THE BEST"; Section II —

"*KNOW* THE LAWS"; Section III — "*DO* THE JOB."

Section I, "*BE* THE BEST," is presented from the employer's point of view, and states the requirements you need to fulfill to become a valuable employee. The chapters "Performance Standards," "Solving Problems," and "Attitude Management" are designed to show you what is expected of you in order to increase your value to the company, and what changes are necessary in order to reach your potential.

Clearly, not everyone in the work force is, or even wants to be, a "best" employee. In fact, some people will always accept life as it is and just try to get by. No matter how simply or factually new ideas are presented, these people just won't try; or they will rationalize that their lot in life is fixed because of a limitation, or because their belief in better conditions is limited. But there is a vast majority of employees who want to do better and would like to be considered among the best. The only thing holding these people back is lack of the knowledge of what to do, and lack of the confidence to do it. Section I will give you that knowledge and instill that confidence.

Reality may appear to encompass only the physical world, but you should recognize that there are unseen dimensions to reality. The physical world behaves according to natural laws which are invisible, but real. In a similar manner, human accomplishments can be traced back to the natural laws of human endeavor. Section II, *"KNOW THE LAWS,"* will give you the theory underlying these natural laws. When you understand and accept the reality of the *Creativity Laws, Compensation Laws,* and *Growth Laws,* success secrets used by countless people through the ages will be a part of your consciousness.

Silent and mighty laws — laws set in motion with great precision and order — work continuously and tirelessly whether or not you choose to acknowledge them. You understand that there are laws of nature that control the pull of gravity, the tides of the sea, the revolution of the earth, and the power of the sun. You also understand the natural laws of the vegetable kingdom. You accept the laws that make a plant grow, a flower bloom, and a seed start the process over again. But do you admit or even understand that the same natural laws that govern nature also govern *your every thought and action?*

Human behavior and all resultant achievements work according to law in the same fashion that all events occur in our Universe. Just as there are natural physical laws, there are also natural laws of human endeavor. Human effort to achieve and advance is possible because the relationships among people, events, and circumstances have a perfect order recognized as law. You may choose to be in harmony with law, which is positive, or you may choose to be in conflict with law and suffer the consequences. Whether you benefit or suf-

fer from law depends largely on your ability to
understand it. You hold the key to that happy
ending or unfortunate conclusion. The frustrations and disappointments you may have experienced in the past are due to your choices, not the
failure of law.

For example, the Law of Gravity never fails. If
an airplane loses its engine power and the wing
velocity reduces to below the stall speed, the airplane will glide downward, because the gross
weight of the plane will be greater than the lifting
force of the airfoil design of the wings. Failure of
the airplane to stay in the air is not a failure of the
law but the failure of the engine to maintain adequate air speed. In like manner, if you experience
a failure in some form of human relations with
another, you must accept the fact that law did not
fail. Attracting cooperation or receiving hostile re-
jections from a business associate is predictable
because behavior works in accord with law.

You must also understand that law is no respecter of persons. For example, if Donald Trump
were to fall off a ten-story building, he would suffer as much harm as you or I would. Law applies
to *all* people, not just chosen individuals. The
same is true of the laws of human endeavor. Because the natural laws of human endeavor are not
respecters of persons, be assured that if even one
person has ever achieved enjoyment, success, and
happiness, then you can, too. Section II defines

the natural laws that turn your daily efforts into enormous successes.

Career building is a continuous process, but through both progression and regression. Your objective is to accelerate your positive progress by leveraging your time and mental efforts daily. It is to your advantage to concentrate your attention on the priorities that will produce the results and outcomes that you desire. Section III, "*DO* THE JOB," will give you a "how-to" philosophy that you can use daily to change your business life for the better. Presenting the "Working for Success" Plan, the chapters "Think," "Work," and "Serve" outline the specific actions that can increase your mental capacity.

Mental capacity is best described as the thinking processes, memory, aptitude, and thinking skill of an individual. An individual's mental capacity is a consciousness defined by two states: professional growth and personal development. Professional growth is that state of an individual's *abilities* as a business person. Personal development is that state of an individual's *character.* In each case, the state of consciousness can be raised when the individual learns how. Through the means of proven techniques and exercise, employees can use the natural laws of human endeavor to increase their mental capacity. With increases in mental capacity, a higher level of job performance is possible, which leads to greater accom-

OVERVIEW

The **BENEFITS** You Seek		
Enjoyable Job Conditions	Career Success	Personal Happiness

TANGIBLE CONDITIONS

MENTAL ACTIVITY

SEC. I	Your Job **ACCOMPLISHMENTS**		
"BE THE BEST"	Job Performance Chapter 1	Problem-Solving Chapter 2	Positive Attitude Chapter 3

SEC. II	Silent & Mighty **LAWS** at Work		
"KNOW THE LAWS"	Creativity Laws Chapter 4	Compensation Laws Chapter 5	Growth Laws Chapter 6

SEC. III	Your Daily **EFFORT** (How-To's)		
"DO THE JOB"	THINK Chapter 7	WORK Chapter 8	SERVE Chapter 9

plishments. These accomplishments will be recognized and rewarded in terms of benefits desired by the employee.

The benefits you seek — enjoyable job conditions, career success, and personal happiness — can be yours in proportion to your mental capacity to perform and to accomplish goals. This mental capacity gives you the power to set into motion the laws which govern your job accomplishments. Section III is designed to help you concentrate on the methods that can expand your mental capacity and give you more successful experiences at work and throughout your professional career.

Looking back over the years, your career milestones establish a trend that could be used as one possible indicator of what your lot in life will be in the future. A more pro-active method is to look within yourself to discover the right career plan for you, then launch out to work the plan, and finally, find your place in the business world — acknowledge your rightful and chosen destiny!

SECTION I

BE THE BEST

Employers want to hire, promote, and keep valuable employees. When making personnel decisions about placement, promotions, and pay increases, employers recognize and reward the employees who contribute most to the company's success. The best employees are set apart from the rest by their *job performance, problem-solving ability,* and *attitude.*

CHAPTER 1
Performance Standards

Jim came into my office one day and said, "Boss, I need a raise. Joan is expecting a baby and we need a new place to live, one with more bedrooms. What's the chance I can have a raise?" I answered, "What? Change your pay because you *want* more money?" Jim continued, "I work hard and I do my job. A raise is only fair." Then I said, "Your compensation today and in the future will be equivalent to the state of your professional growth and personal development. You must first *be* before you *get*." Jim looked a little annoyed. I went on to say, "Sit down, Jim, and let's discuss what you can do to *earn* a raise."

Top management people in American business generally agree that one of the key factors in developing a smoothly-functioning and efficient organization is the full utilization of its human resources. The performance of the individual employee is essential to achieve the strategies and plans of the owners. At the same time, the employee's performance fulfills his/her own primary objectives of professional growth and personal development, and his/her need to earn an income. Employer and employee can work in harmony to achieve goals important to both.

The Formula for Performance

The usual *main* goal of business owners is to make an acceptable profit, commensurate with the risk of the business and the the resources they have invested in it. (Acquiring enough income to cover expenses is the goal of a charity and of a government agency, and earning a fixed profit is the goal of a monopoly.) In whatever business you are in, taking in income greater than expenses (profit-making) will be important to your employer. Employers and employees have the opportunity to work together to serve customers and to achieve the financial results desired by the corporate owners.

How well the business organization performs its mission to produce profits will be primarily dependent upon the interaction of employees in delivering a total output which is greater than the sum of the individual contributions. Thus, it stands to reason that each employee's job accomplishments make an important contribution to the success or failure of the business. Also, it is reasonable to assume that achievers who consistently demonstrate high performance are likely to accomplish more and enjoy more recognition than employees who do average work. Which would you prefer to have with you in your foxhole, on your project team, in your department, on the board of directors — "The Achiever" or "Mr. Average"?

Performance is a measurement of an employee's accomplishments made possible by his/her state of professional growth and personal development. In order to assist the development of employees, most businesses have either formal or informal performance measurement techniques. Through this process, the employee's professional growth and personal development can be nurtured by the employer. Helping employees to be more aware of deficiencies and recognizing their accomplishments is a form of coaching that benefits both the employee and the employer. It is through performance measurement that achievers become identified as "best" employees.

Whether consciously or not, business managers evaluate employees' contributions by universal performance standards. Although the exact procedures will vary by company or individual manager, the components of an employee's performance will be similar. Concentrating on these components and improving any weak areas increases the likelihood that an employee's performance will improve, thereby increasing the value of his/her contribution. If you wish your employer would appreciate your work and contribution more, then the components making up your job performance must be a priority in your business life.

When examining employee performance objectively, you will discover that job accomplishments have their roots in activities relating to technical abilities, personal drive, and people skills. The Formula for Performance breaks these "root" activities down into components that can be managed for better success. The Formula for Performance has three components: *competence, commitment* and *cooperation*. The performance level achieved by an employee is simply the sum of these components.

PERFORMANCE = COMPETENCE +
                        COMMITMENT + COOPERATION

The best employees will have strength in each component as well as balance among all three. When the level of each component is high, then the resultant performance output will be the highest possible.

Similarly, an unbalanced relationship will result in lower overall performance. For example, one can be highly competent in a field of work but lack personal commitment or a cooperative attitude towards others. A technically competent employee may be assigned a job which strongly emphasizes the need for technical skills, and may do very well at it. Even so, this employee will accomplish more and become more versatile if he/she demonstrates high levels of commitment and cooperation in addition to competence.

The Competence Component

Making informed and accurate choices, decisions, and judgments every day is the *Competence*

Component. Competence is the ability to recognize, analyze, and diagnose problems, evaluate facts, and exercise good judgment in arriving at sensible and practical solutions. Competence demands know-how, expertise, and talent. The Competence Component chart on page 30 identifies the elements and proficiencies contributing to the Competence Component of Performance. As you can see, to be competent means to have great knowledge and skill in a trade or profession, derived from education, training, practice, and experience.

The elements of Knowledge and Skill are not natural abilities, but learned qualities which have been developed through study (concentration) and exercise. This learning experience is made possible by the means of one's mental capacity, which is best described as thinking processes, memory, aptitude, and thinking skill. Your inborn intellect and talent, and the experience you gain through life, both play a role in the learning process of acquiring Knowledge and Skill.

For some, high levels of competence come early because of inborn aptitudes, or opportunities for formal education or practical training. Others achieve high levels of competence later in life due to extensive practice or experience. Although natural aptitude can give one an early advantage, the eventual level of competence one achieves is primarily due to study (concentration) and exercise. Remember the times when you took a class in college or trade school? In order to ac-

COMPETENCE COMPONENT

Structure

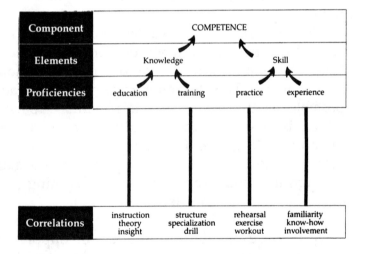

quire new knowledge or develop a new skill, you had to study and do exercises that led you through the course right up to the final examination. It is this type of mental exercise that develops mental capacity and impresses learning experiences into the mind. High levels of competence will be the observed behavior of the employees who are mentally prepared.

Knowledge about one's field is a major qualification for professional jobs. Degrees and Certificates are desired by many employers primarily because these documents prove that the prospective employee has acquired knowledge, and can be assumed to be an individual committed to learning. But Knowledge is only half of the Competence Component. Successful performance is only possible when Knowledge is put into practice as a Skill.

When I graduated from college and started my first job, I was prepared academically. I soon received specialized training in the business practices and operations of my employer. Within six months of my start date, I could consider myself knowledgeable, but still a long way from being truly competent. It took a couple of years of working at my job to develop the meaningful skills necessary to be effective in my assignments. My decision-making, communications, problem-solving, and time management skills improved to some degree with each experience. I built up my competence slowly at first, but the subsequent years of acquiring new knowledge and new skills raised my competence steadily, year after year.

Competent employees are usually experts in their organization on a particular subject or area of the business. Their Knowledge and Skill are respected. You can probably identify one or more associates at your place of work that you consider to be experts. Those individuals may be the ones who are always assigned the tough technical problems or invited to meetings when professional advice is needed. They are competent.

You have seen how the Competence Component is structured, and observed a few examples of competent people at your work place. However, it is entirely possible that the people you have selected as competent employees may have differing levels of performance. Some just don't get things done, or they fail to help others in a supportive manner. Competence alone is not enough; the *Commitment Component* and the *Cooperation Component* of performance are of equal importance if the total performance is to be the highest possible.

The Commitment Component

Personal determination to do the job is the *Commitment Component*. Commitment is setting a goal as a top priority, and failure to accomplish that goal is not considered an alternative. When a

Navy plane is launched from an aircraft carrier, the plane is committed. The pilot can't stop the aircraft after the catapult fires. Any uncertainty the pilot may have about the aircraft's ability to fly will have to be ignored because he is now personally committed, and there is only one way to go — UP! Like it or not, the pilot is committed to flying the plane to achieve the mission.

In the business world, commitment is a pledge of maximum effort to accomplish a mission. The mission becomes the predominant goal that all energies are focused upon. With commitment comes the possibility of failure, but genuine commitment leaves little room for this likelihood. Setbacks and disappointments are thought of as temporary conditions, because there are more ways than one to get a job done. With the vision of the mission being accomplished, commitment focuses efforts and energies on success, not failure. Commitment is a mental attitude.

The Commitment Component chart on page 34 identifies the elements and traits contributing to the Commitment Component of Performance. To be committed means to have Confidence and Motivation to perform a task or achieve success. Commitment is the inspiring dimension of an individual that combines the traits of belief, self-assurance, interest, and enthusiasm into action.

The level of commitment is determined by an individual's feelings about the mission or the job to be done. The perceptions and thoughts held by

COMMITMENT COMPONENT
Structure

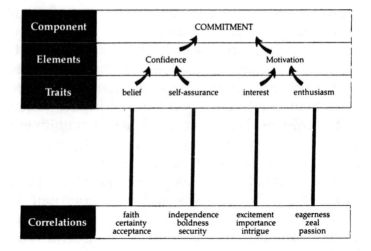

the individual rule over decisions to either launch out maximum effort or hold back half-heartedly. What one believes to be true, and what one is interested in, play a significant role in raising the level of commitment.

When John F. Kennedy declared on May 25, 1961, that America would land an astronaut on the moon before the end of the decade, he was making a personal commitment to the mission. He *believed* it was technically possible; the scientists and engineers of NASA and contractors gave him a feeling of *self-assurance;* the anticipated economic growth of the country propelled his *interest;* and his vision of the accomplishment intensified his *enthusiasm.* President Kennedy's commitment inspired and motivated an entire nation and captured the world's imagination. The space program achieved the highest possible performance level. Neil Armstrong's "small step" on the moon's surface was July 20, 1969. The objective was achieved!

Commitment in the workplace must be just as bold as President Kennedy's commitment. The magnitude of some commitments may be different, but the personal involvement in making and keeping commitments should be of the same intensity. Ultimately, accomplishment of a production goal, a financial objective, or a solution to a problem will be directly proportionate to the intensity of mental powers committed to the cause. Over a span of a decade, 500,000 scientists, bureaucrats, and engineers were committed to the moon landing objective!

Most employees do not realize that commitment is a creative force. It is this component of performance that gets things done, and in a timely manner. Commitment is the catalyst which can turn Competence and Cooperation into execution and accomplishment!

The Cooperation Component

Harmonious interaction with other people is the *Cooperation Component*. Individual contributions, if isolated, will produce one set of results. But when each employee freely extends himself/herself to help an associate, individual outputs are leveraged dramatically. When employees cooperate, if one associate makes a mistake or misunderstands some vital communication, another employee can provide "make-up" support with minimal effort or interruption. Thus, cooperation produces a sum greater than parts. The combined contributions keep the performance of the organization high.

The Cooperation Component chart on page 38 identifies the elements and traits that contribute to the Cooperation Component of Performance. To be cooperative means to show Helpfulness and Admiration toward others. The spirit in which an employee extends himself/herself with positive traits of supportiveness, willingness, respectfulness, and submissiveness helps to contribute to the success of others while accomplishing the goals of the employer. Cooperation is a mental attitude.

The level of cooperation is determined by an individual's attitude toward others and himself/herself. How one views the importance of other people is likely to cause judgments about how to treat others. These judgments influence how one uses his/her abilities, talents, and resources for the benefit of another.

How can you spot a cooperative associate? Words like, "I'll take on that assignment," or, "It's not my job," usually are dead giveaways. In most organizations, it is fairly easy to identify the team players and to isolate the self-centered loners. The team player works cooperatively, communicates openly, and is friendly. The self-centered loner is usually grumpy, belligerent, or indifferent. In both cases, the level of total performance will be proportionate to the level of cooperation.

In every organization I have ever worked in, I have worked with "personality mavericks" — people who seem to have chips on their shoulders or to feel so insecure that they are continuously on an emotional roller coaster. Many are considered competent technical experts, and some may have high levels of commitment. In almost all

COOPERATION COMPONENT

Structure

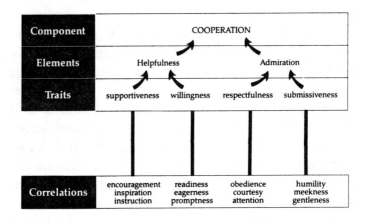

cases, however, they will demonstrate low total performance due to their difficulty with the Cooperation Component. The "sour apple" effect created by such insensitive people is likely to inject a disruptive force into any organization. What these individuals do not understand or choose to ignore is that cooperation is important. Cooperation brings Competence and Commitment into the mainstream of the employer's business.

Measurement of the Total Performance

Is your performance acceptable to your employer, and do you think it is the best it could be? Before you can start to make positive changes for the future, you must understand how well you are performing your job today. By using the Performance Review Form on page 40, you can evaluate yourself. Rate yourself as honestly as you can on each of the 12 fundamental attributes. (As a guide, think of the "best" possible level possessed by others in your department, company, or business community as the standard for a score of ten.) Then simply add up your score and transfer the sums to the blanks provided. You will have to make some judgments in rating yourself, but your actual score is not as important as is the general indication of strong and weak areas. I offer this technique merely as a device to help you work systematically at your own performance.

PERFORMANCE REVIEW FORM

score 0–10:
10 highest

Proficiencies	Elements	Components

1. education _____
2. training + _____

SubT _____ → _____ Knowledge

3. practice _____
4. experience + _____

SubT _____ →+ _____ Skill

SubT _____ → _____ COMPETENCE

Traits

5. belief _____
6. self-assurance + _____

SubT _____ → _____ Confidence

7. interest _____
8. enthusiasm + _____

SubT _____ →+ _____ Motivation

SubT _____ →+ _____ COMMITMENT

9. supportiveness _____
10. willingness + _____

SubT _____ → _____ Helpfulness

11. respectfulness _____
12. submissiveness + _____

SubT _____ →+ _____ Admiration

SubT _____ →+ _____ COOPERATION

Performance
Rating
_____

Your final score is your performance rating, which is an indication of your overall performance. Compare this score to the Performance Standard on page 42 to find out how you stack up if you work in an "average" American corporation. The score ranges presented for each rating classification are, from my experience, typical. (The Performance Rating Definitions on page 44 may help you to have a better understanding of the various levels of performance.) If your score was lower than you would like, look at the specific attributes on which you gave yourself a low score. Visualize how your performance rating could change if you successfully improved in just one attribute!

At one point in my career I was placed in a job assignment that was not to my liking. Clearly, I was qualified and could make a significant contribution, but I just wasn't excited about the circumstances. Although these feelings of dissatisfaction did not have a factual basis, I initially perceived that the job was not a good move. The job was very similar to one I had held years earlier, and I felt my career was being side-tracked. Since I did not have a well-thought-out career plan at the time, and I needed the income, I accepted the assignment.

After many months, I still didn't have my heart in the job. I rated my progress using the Performance Review Form.

PERFORMANCE STANDARD

Rating Ranges

RATING	SCORE RANGE	("Average" Company) DISTRIBUTION OF WORK FORCE
OUTSTANDING	114–120	5%
EXCELLENT	100–113	10%
GOOD	64–99	30%
AVERAGE	16–63	40%
MARGINAL	4–15	10%
POOR	0–3	5%

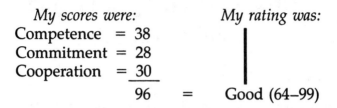

My scores were:		*My rating was:*
Competence	= 38	
Commitment	= 28	
Cooperation	= 30	
	96 =	Good (64–99)

My lack of interest and my stubborn will resulted in a lower performance score than that which was possible. I wasn't doing my best work, and I overlooked how this job could give me knowledge that would benefit my professional growth and personal development. I now realize that I was creating negative job conditions, stress, and unhappiness by not coming to grips with the problem of my performance. Meanwhile, I sensed that my supervisor and associates also viewed my performance as merely GOOD.

How could I reach my potential? Some things had to change. For a three-month period, I used the technique called QUIET (described in a later chapter) to concentrate on the attitude traits for which I had a low score — *interest* in the job, and *submissiveness* to my company's needs at that time. Through this transformation period, the job took on a new meaning, because I started to see how I could improve my state of professional growth and personal development from the experience. Although I wasn't receiving instant gratification, I could begin to see positive possibilities of how to perform the job better and how to help myself become a better businessman. My perception about

PERFORMANCE RATING DEFINITIONS

OUTSTANDING

Recognized expert; self-supervised; gets job done effectively; positive contributor; thinks broadly about objectives; ready for promotion.

EXCELLENT

Accomplishes more than expected; occasional supervision required; thinks beyond detail; works toward department objectives; normally considered for promotion.

GOOD

Few errors (seldom repeated); usually completes work and schedules on time; good team player; normally a positive influence on others.

AVERAGE

Has proven capability; doing satisfactory job; shows initiative and drive; needs to acquire more "know-how" to improve rating.

MARGINAL

Causing morale problem; on job long enough to show better performance; seems to be mistake-prone; often repeating the same errors.

POOR

Not capable of doing job; quantity, quality, and timeliness of work do not meet expectations; negative impact on department; detriment to the organization.

the assignment began to change, and my attitude became more positive.

As the three-month period closed, I was more interested in the business, and my communications with associates were improving as well. My involvement in special projects and customer relations issues helped the organization to achieve better performance results. Interruptions to my schedule seemed to be less stressful than they had in the past. I was doing a better job of setting a leadership example for my employees. On more than one occasion, an associate would volunteer a remark such as, "You must be having a good day." I was feeling better about myself, my circumstances -- and it was showing!

I felt that I was making progress, but in order to be sure, I repeated my performance review. To my delight, Commitment came up to 38 and Cooperation reached 34, for a total of 110 — a rating of EXCELLENT with the real potential of reaching OUTSTANDING! I was getting more work done, I was learning more about building a successful business, and I liked the direction in which I was heading. My job became more enjoyable, my career got on track, and my supervisor gave me high marks on my next "official" performance review. My job conditions did change for the better.

The effort is worth it, for employers want and will keep those employees who are OUTSTANDING and EXCELLENT performers. These employees find satisfying work, earn higher salaries, and get promotions. Employees rated in the GOOD and AVERAGE range will have jobs, but growth in those jobs will be slow in coming. Also, in economic down-swings, these employees are more likely to be let go if the employer is forced to reduce the labor force. Employees rated in the MARGINAL and POOR ranges are either in the wrong job or are not yet prepared to handle the job. Each employee can take control of his/her performance and make himself/herself a better performer.

Performance Can Be Improved

Good job placements, promotions, and pay increases are assured if the performance contribution of the employee is valuable to the employer. Like Jim, who wanted a raise, each employee can earn recognition and rewards if there is continued improvement in performance. This need for greater performance will always exist, and it can be fulfilled by concentrating on the mental attitude characteristics of the components of Performance: Competence, Commitment, and Cooperation.

As you have now seen, the first step in improving performance is to understand the structure making up the components of Performance. The second step is to recognize where you are right now in regard to your performance. The third step is to launch a personal program to strengthen the weak areas of your performance as a means to achieve the highest possible total performance. *Performance can be improved.*

It is your job performance that leads to accomplishments. Remember, your employer needs you to accomplish the strategies and goals of the company. It is accomplishing those strategies and goals that makes the employer successful. Working to raise your state of professional growth and personal development (mental capacity) increases the likelihood that your performance will improve, thereby giving your employer accomplishments that are worthy of recognition and compensation. With the right kind of effort, you can be one of the best employees that your employer could wish for!

CHAPTER 2
Solving Problems

Norman Vincent Peale tells about being stopped on the streets of New York by a man who said, "Reverend, I've got problems!" Dr. Peale answered, "Well, I know a place near here that has a population of fifteen thousand people, and not a person has a problem." His troubled friend said, "Tell me, where is this place? I'd like to live there." And Dr. Peale answered, "It's Woodlawn Cemetery in the Bronx!"

Dr. Peale has said that problems are a sign of life; if you have a lot of problems, then you are really alive. You will be faced with many problems on your journey along the success trail. The way you cope with and react to problems will set you apart from others, so get ready to develop your problem-solving skills and learn how to remain calm during the interruptions caused by problems. Be reassured; problem-solving skills will *always* be needed in American business.

The Nature of Business Problems

Understanding the nature of problems that cause business performance disappointments and low employee morale is a desirable accomplishment. The "best" employees recognize the existence of the root problems and know how to solve them permanently. If the "root problems" (*real* causes) are not solved, they will cause business failures and lost jobs. Eventually, the business problems of your employer will affect you, and the way in which you handle problems will contribute to the success or failure of your employer. Good problem-solvers know where to look to find the root problems and the best solutions.

The results of root business problems are manifested in ways that many people mistake for the problems themselves — lost sales, poor product quality, late deliveries, poor profits, increased employee absenteeism, low employee morale, high warranty expense, and excessive customer complaints. Typically, the "problems" of the business appear complex and difficult to fix. But all of these negative business concerns are not problems. They are SYMPTOMS!

Your job may be full of difficult and persistent dilemmas that seem impossible to solve. Mistakes, last-minute surprises, missed commitments, and miscommunications by others may have caused difficulties in performing your job. At times, it may appear that things are getting worse instead of better. These negative job conditions are not problems. They are SYMPTOMS!

Much of the daily effort of managers and employees is focused upon only the symptoms of root problems. A symptom is a dilemma observed as a negative business concern or negative employee behavior. Many times, frustration and stress are experienced by one who is confronted with a dilemma. How simple life would be if we could just find one magical solution that works for all dilemmas! All disappointments, interruptions, negative performances, predicaments, and embarrassments would be fixed by the stroke of a wand! Unfortunately, there is no magical solution. To solve a dilemma permanently, the root problem first has to be identified.

If negative concerns and behaviors are only symptoms identified as dilemmas, then what are the root problems to be solved? There are basically five root problems to deal with when improving business performance and job conditions. The root problems to solve are centered in the mental realm and deal with LEADERSHIP, MOTIVATION, COMMUNICATIONS, CHANGE, and PRODUCTIVITY. These areas of human endeavor become problems when their importance is ignored or not addressed in a timely manner. These problems work both independently and in combination as the underlying causes for *all* business- and job-related dilemmas.

By being sensitive to the "hidden" nature of each of these problems and by working to discover which problem(s) is the root cause of your particular dilemma(s), you can contribute to permanent solutions and increase your skill to help others overcome dilemmas. Most employees will not perceive the invisible root problems, and so

THE ROOT PROBLEMS
LEADERSHIP
MOTIVATION
COMMUNICATIONS
CHANGE
PRODUCTIVITY

will be completely unaware of how to solve them permanently. It is to your advantage to recognize which one (or more) of the root problems causes a specific dilemma you are facing. Look at the outer manifestation of the dilemma, recognize that what you see is only a symptom, identify the root problem, and set about to work out a solution that solves the root problem permanently.

The Leadership Problem

A truly exceptional business leader possesses the mental qualities of awareness, desire, initiative, decisiveness, courage, and objectivity. Those who have leadership roles — corporate managers, product managers, sales managers, departmental supervisors, project leaders — must possess strength in these qualities if they hope to have growing and successful careers. But what most employees don't realize is that *everyone* in the organization — whatever his/her role — is expected to develop and use his/her leadership qualities, too.

In accomplishing even the simplest task, each employee will exhibit various leadership styles and proficiencies. Many employees won't think of themselves as leaders, while some may demonstrate outstanding leadership skills. It is the poor quality of leadership throughout the organization that may cause business and job dilemmas lead-

ing to business failures and personal disappointments. In your own performance and the
performance of your associates and superiors,
watch for these five qualities of leadership: awareness, desire, initiative, decisiveness, courage, and
objectivity.

1. *AWARENESS* — the ability to sense what is going on
about you. Have your "antenna" out so you can receive
signals that indicate when trouble may be brewing. Lo-
cate and address mistakes before they become full-
blown crises.
2. *DESIRE* — the determination to accomplish the goal.
Determination keeps you focused on the most important tasks. Your goals may be business-oriented or of a
personal nature, but, in either case, mental commitment
is strong enough to see those goals accomplished.
3. *INITIATIVE* — determining what needs to be done
and taking steps to see that it is done. Great leaders ini-
tiate actions without being told. Even if the path isn't
easy, these leaders cause things to happen long before
most people even realize that action is required.
4. *DECISIVENESS* — the ability to make choices. Intel-
ligent decisions result from investigating the facts, listening intently, thinking constructively, and deciding
rationally. Although research may be necessary for some
decisions, it is important to reach decisions quickly and
implement them at once. Then you can allow adequate
time to evaluate the results of the new course before
making further changes.
5. *COURAGE* — the backbone to do the right thing.
When a mistake is made, be willing to admit responsibility and do what is necessary to correct the situation.
Facing problems squarely and daring to do the right
thing takes courage.

6. *OBJECTIVITY* — the discipline to look at business, jobs, and personnel circumstances without letting previous biases or personal emotions and impulses rule your actions. Setting high standards for yourself and those you supervise, and using facts as the basis for decisions, signifies a leader who has the discipline to be objective.

Some dilemmas caused by the leadership problem may become apparent quickly. For example, a decision made without using common sense may get immediate reactions from others: criticizing an associate in public or writing a negative memo to his/her boss will likely have a negative effect on cooperation; letting a customer complaint wait until tomorrow may result in a more unpleasant confrontation later; throwing a temper tantrum may alienate associates and customers; missing a scheduled commitment even by one day may cause a significant delay in an important project. The organization's effectiveness can be adversely affected by the poor leadership of one or more members of the group.

On the other hand, the leadership problem may be disguised so that it takes a long time before adverse conditions become apparent. Leaders at the top are in charge of decisions that have a far-reaching impact on a company's success and future achievements. For example, not being aware of world economic trends may create a financial dilemma in a few years; picking the wrong product strategy may place the company in a noncompetitive position in the market place; se-

88

lecting personnel on the basis of their looks or their friendships will certainly lead to dilemmas. Whether quickly or over the long run, the leadership problem will have its effects on business performance.

The Motivation Problem

The problem of motivation is one that exists at one level or another in every organization. When employees are not interested in the job or enthusiastic about the work, their performance becomes less than desirable. Low motivation levels lead to negative attitudes, carelessness, and errors. The symptoms of tardiness, increasing absenteeism, low morale, and poor product quality soon follow. Thus, lack of motivation detracts from the overall performance of the organization.

You will know motivated employees by the interest and enthusiasm they demonstrate in the tasks they undertake and accomplish. Motivation is an internally-generated stimulus, powered by ideas and topics that intrigue and excite. For example, having the opportunity to get involved with computers may help to motivate some employees. Challenges and opportunities to learn or to demonstrate skills can motivate many employees, particularly if they are presented in a manner that is personalized. It is important for you to discover what arouses the interest and enthusiasm of those you supervise; knowing what excites your own interest and enthusiasm helps.

Company leaders also help to increase employee motivation by being informative about important data. Employees want to know what's expected of them, where they stand in the company, how they can progress in their jobs, and how they can increase their salaries. Also, management is responsible for extending support, encouragement, and recognition, which ignite the employee's internal motivation. A successful leader supplies this information in terms the employee can understand.

I was impressed with the McDonnell Douglas Corporation chairman's method of motivating his 20,000-plus employees in St. Louis. James S. McDonnell, "Mr. Mac," would come on the public address system any time good news or developments were happening. One day I was walking through the F4 Phantom fighter production line, and over the PA I heard, "This is Mac calling the team. This is Mac calling the team." The entire production line came to a halt and the employees listened as he told us about booking orders for the new DC10 commercial aircraft. As I recall, he finished the announcement with the words, "That's a lot of bread and butter!" Our future depended upon the success of the introduction of this product. As employees, we felt good about the news,

and we felt important because Mr. Mac personally
informed us of the progress in getting early orders.

An organization with employees who do not
possess intense internal motivation is an organization that is doomed. Even a few poorly-
motivated employees can cause an organization to
fall short. In most cases, the poorly-motivated
employees need help recognizing how their behavior is affecting both their work and the overall
performance of the organization. One-on-one
coaching may put things into perspective and re-
direct such employees.

I had the experience of observing an employee
who was truly qualified for his job, but didn't
seem motivated to work very hard at it. In meetings, he would look distant or be cleaning his fin-
gernails while important issues were being
discussed. At times, when action was required of
this employee, he would work at other tasks less
important. His lack of action resulted in lost man-
hours and material waste. After my urging for
more involvement and better results seemed to
fail, we met in my office to discuss the future. Together, we identified the source of his low motivation level — he didn't like the kind of work he
was doing. In three months' time, this employee
was transferred to another department and was
assigned a job that he was truly interested in.
Shortly after the transfer, he demonstrated interest in everything affecting his job, and he became

aggressive in his pursuit to accomplish high priority goals. This employee was now *motivated!*

The individual employee's performance is affected either positively or negatively in proportion to his/her internal motivation level. As pointed out in Chapter 1, motivation has a great deal to do with the Commitment Component of Performance. Some business dilemmas, such as late projects and missed commitments, can be traced back to the motivational level of the employees involved. The motivation problem affects the employee's performance and thereby influences the business performance of the employer.

The Communications Problem

We must accept the proposition that no two people can ever completely grasp a meaning in the same way. Meaning is a very private affair. Individuals cannot have identical experience in any given situation. It is always possible for an associate to say they understand what you said and meant, but in reality, they may perceive the message in a completely different form than what you intended. Accepting this concept encourages us to seek ways to clarify messages and avoid placing blame for miscommunications on the other person.

The impact of miscommunications can be significant. Whether misunderstandings occur in commercial contracts or routine inter-office memos, the result is waste — in direct dollars, lost man-hours, and missed opportunities. Therefore, both verbal and written communications must be clear. When agreements and important discussions are not written down, it is possible for people's memories to lose track of the decisions made or the actions assigned. Miscommunications waste energies and resources.

The communications problem can exist during the routine activities of each day. For example, my parts buyer issued monthly orders to one of our major suppliers. Each month, most of the parts were late, and, therefore, Production shipped some critical orders late to our customers. Expediting parts and expending overtime in production became a way of life. Then we discovered the root problem. The buyer would place the parts order, the supplier would confirm a delivery date for each part, then our buyer accepted the dates and notified Production of the pending availability. The problem came when the supplier had dilemmas that affected his deliveries, but he did not notify our buyer of the delay. If the supplier *had* notified us, our production people could have elected to reschedule the customer order, or located the needed parts from another supplier. Communications weren't working. It was a communications problem causing our extra costs and customer dissatisfaction.

Each new business concept introduced to a company represents a potential dilemma which can be eased by effective communications. Some examples of these new business concepts are:

1. new technological developments and products,
2. relocation of the business to another city,
3. new business systems and office computers,
4. leveraged buy-outs of companies,
5. reduction of middle-management staffing,
6. consolidation of companies within an industry.

These and other business concepts demand that management and employees talk with each other. Exchanging information freely helps to avoid negative perceptions by the employees involved. As you are involved in projects and assignments, always ask yourself who should be notified or consulted in regard to decisions you make. Errors occur when one assumes the "word" will get to the right person. Extra effort spent on communications will produce better results. Successful business performance is possible when the communications problem is addressed early.

The Change Problem

Change is inevitable. The world economy and the American economy are always changing. American business must change in order to stay abreast of its competition. Every year, changes come more frequently and with greater intensity. Just as problems will always be part of any human endeavor, change will be with us throughout our careers. Although change is a constant challenge, specific problems caused by change can be identified and resolved permanently.

Change is a major business problem because the symptoms are so far-reaching. For example, delays brought about by product switch-over may allow a competitor to get ahead in the market place; inaccurate accounting data from a new computer may cause product to be sold at the wrong price; new products and the training of new personnel may cause disruption in a smooth-running operation. What was routine before will take more time and, possibly, waste some materials until any change process is complete.

The word "change" evokes fear and pain in the subconscious of most people. They believe that with change comes instability. Changes in work assignments, work methods, or work procedures mean that the individual must work harder to learn about new technology, products, organizations, or projects. The mind that fears and resists change becomes paralyzed and ceases to have ideas of its own, because the mind can only concentrate on one thing at a time.

Resistance to change should be expected because everyone finds comfort in what is familiar and consistent with his/her thinking patterns. Also, the natural tendency to do what is easy makes people want to avoid the dilemmas anticipated with making a change. When change is not accepted by an employee, wasted energy and efforts will occur. For instance, employees may invent excuses to explain why things are going wrong instead of digging in and getting the job done. These employees are not acknowledging their mental resistance to a dictated change.

The Productivity Problem

In order to be competitive today, American businesses need to produce a greater volume of products and services, with decreasing inputs of labor and material, while improving quality. But these productivity requirements are compromised when the business is plagued with symptoms such as duplicate shipments, lost documents, complicated product designs, poor engineering documentation, long order-processing delays, and lack of accurate information. All of these created dilemmas usually take extra labor and/or material to resolve.

Productivity is the problem if more and more people are needed to do the work when profits are becoming less and less abundant. If a step-up in output is required, there is usually a tendency to add more labor. Adding staff may indeed increase capacity, but, unless properly directed, the extra man-hours may only add extra cost without achieving a proportionate increase in output. Employees will accomplish what is required of them in whatever time period they are given. If the

time period is too short, the quality of the work
will suffer. If too much time is given, time will be
wasted because there is a natural tendency to fill
the time available. Extended schedules and excessive labor and material costs may indicate the existence of a productivity problem.

The productivity problem is a drain on the energies and efforts of all employees in the company. Improved productivity will result in a better
place to work, better company financial performance, and better customer service. With competitive pressures in the market place for higher
quality and lower prices, the need to minimize
the productivity problem is paramount for the
business to be successful.

Seeing the Root Problem

You now know the five problems that cause all
business- and job-related dilemmas. The Common Dilemmas chart on page 66 presents a few of
the problems found frequently in businesses. The
chart offers some possible mental contributors behind each problem, and you can see that when
these contributors are understood, the solution to
the root problem becomes apparent. This knowledge gives you an edge. With some practice, you
can think objectively about the symptoms you observe, identify the root problem, and implement

an effective solution to solve the problem permanently.

For example, as part of a business acquisition, I once had the job of transforming a custom manufacturing operation from a financial ruin to a successful star in the corporation. The business had been in a financial slump for several years. The symptoms I observed were noncompetitive products, low employee morale, poor financial results, and customer complaints. In addition, the sales and service channel needed reassurance that the business was going to continue. Fortunately, there was a market need for the equipment. Careful analysis verified that three root problems were the bases of the unfavorable business performance.

First, MOTIVATION was a problem because the employees were tired and frustrated after working hard for several years, yet losing money each year. Returning the business to a profitable operation appeared hopeless. Interest and enthusiasm were down, and creativity and performance contributions of the employees just didn't reach potential. However, the problem of motivation wasn't the key issue.

Second, PRODUCTIVITY was a problem in the office operations of the business. Customer orders were being scheduled and processed through the various departments without the aid of a common data base. Without a central computer, the

COMMON DILEMMAS

Dilemmas Which Are Symptoms	Typical Characteristics	Possible Root Problem	Possible Mental Contributor
Unhappy Customer	angry, disappointed, feels cheated, mis-informed, ignored, desperate	Leadership	lack of focus on customer's needs
Disgruntled Employee	misunderstandings, lack of direction, too much criticism, lack of recognition for effort	Leadership	minimal involve-ment of supervisor
	fear of new assign-ment, unwilling to try something new	Change	employee's lack of self-confidence
Bogged-downed Projects	late completions, indifference to commitments, confused priorities	Leadership	lack of a "cham-pion" to set objectives and follow throug
Drop in Sales	long lead times for product deliveries	Produc-tivity	poor methods & designs
	poor quality	Motivation	lack of atten-tion to details
	confused business mission, prices too high, competitive pressures	Leadership	absence of a strategic plan
Rising Costs	higher vendor prices	Leadership	single source decision
	increased labor requirements	Productivity	poor designs, skills, and/or tools
Technical Problems	poor equipment perfor-mance, high warranty expense	Communi-cations	lack of data, minimal ex-change of idea

clerical handling of countless details resulted in
long delivery cycles, late deliveries, high inven-
tories, costly mistakes, and untimely financial
documentation. Understandably, customer satisfaction was low, and financial results were poor.

To solve the productivity problem, several strategic steps were necessary: (1) Capital was used to
buy a business computer system (office "tool"),
and the employees worked extra hard to implement the business software package while keeping the manual data system operating in parallel;
(2) The organization was restructured to focus on
customer service in office operations and in post-
shipment activities; (3) Special training for some
employees and re-assignment of others to jobs
which provided a better match completed the organization realignment; (4) Stricter guidelines
were established which defined the types of custom projects that would be pursued and which
designs would be used for patterns (product strategy). As a result, designs were easier to manufac-
ture, inventory costs decreased, quality improved,
and, even though prices became higher, customer
satisfaction slowly made favorable progress.

Even with good productivity investments
made, the job wasn't done. The business and
our employees went through numerous changes
during implementation phases; the need for
good communications was never greater. All of
the elements of the problems of CHANGE and
COMMUNICATIONS, such as uncertainty and

misunderstanding, were present throughout the process. These problems were solved by establishing teams with the purpose of managing a specific change while still conducting their day-to-day business. Managers, supervisors, and individuals were assigned special projects in addition to their normal responsibilities. Communications needs of the organization quickly became everyone's responsibility. Small successes became more frequent. Then, at last, we started to make money!

As the business made the turn, the problem of motivation diminished. The employees could finally see positive progress for the business. Also, they soon learned that their contributions were recognized and appreciated. Corporate officials visited the operation and thanked the employees personally for a job well done. Several associates who excelled in their performance during this rebuilding period were promoted; others were awarded salary increases. All the employees shared in improved fringe benefits. The organization became stronger and stronger as the combined efforts and enthusiasm of the employees changed the environment. The business made a cultural change from defeated player to successful performer.

A lot of problem-solving had transpired, but what do you think had been the single most critical problem? There was one root problem that led to the creation of the Motivation and Productivity problems. At the heart was a LEADERSHIP problem. The business needed a management team with strong leadership qualities, that could work together to discover what was needed, and that had the drive to see changes carried out with balance and fairness. With my application of the "Working for Success" Plan, I was successful in bringing a team together which consisted of members that possessed or soon adopted positive leadership qualities. Each leadership quality — awareness, desire, initiative, decisiveness, courage, and objectivity — was involved in the process to improve the financial performance of this business:

1. *desire* to achieve the business turnaround *goal,*
2. *awareness* of the *root problems,*
3. *objectivity* to accurately *evaluate* markets, product lines, and employee performance,
4. *initiative* to define an action *plan,*
5. *decisiveness* to make *choices,*
6. *courage* to *implement* the plan

This business turnaround example deals with common problems plaguing American business organizations. Understanding the root problems was essential in achieving success. Likewise, your job-related problems can be handled more easily when viewed with the five root problems in mind. The difference between a business dilemma and a job-related dilemma is only that of degree. The nature of problems dealing with human endeavors (business and jobs) will be similar in all cases.

Learn to Discover Root Problems

Business- and job-related problems you face may present dilemmas that are frustrating and stressful. However, if you analyze each situation in terms of root problems, you may be surprised to find how simple the solutions really are. When you learn of a dilemma affecting your job, project, or department, look for the unseen causes of the observable symptoms. Determine for yourself whether LEADERSHIP, MOTIVATION, COMMUNICATIONS, CHANGE, or PRODUCTIVITY problems are at the root of the trouble. The best employees will understand what is really happening.

The five root business- and job-related problems all have one common origin: *poor thinking*, characterized by lack of planning, lack of ideas, poor choices, uninformed judgments, procrastination, laziness, mental mistakes, narrow opinions, and ignoring the importance of details. When you realize that problems are imperfections created by poor thinking, you can activate your mental powers to erase the effect of these thoughts. Your mental capacity can be used to direct your steps as you solve your job-related problems and assist superiors and associates in solving business problems. People create problems, and, one way or another, people will solve them.

Each problem you solve will contribute to raising your state of professional growth and personal development. Because of your effort to exercise your mind during the problem-solving process, you will increase your mental capacity with each experience. Ignoring problems or avoiding thinking about the consequences will only leave your mental resources at status quo. But if you really concentrate on identifying and solving root problems, you will find it a skill that can be learned, and solutions will become more easily recognized.

Looking beyond observable symptoms to discover the root problems is a unique skill. Only with this knowledge do you have the advantage many employees overlook: You can help yourself to solve your job-related problems and help your employer solve business problems permanently. Your employer will benefit, from either lower costs or additional sales, in a magnitude proportionate to your success in solving problems. Each and every problem solved will have an influence on the company's success — and on your personal success. So develop this unique skill and use it to accelerate your own professional growth and personal development!

CHAPTER 3
Attitude Management

A product transfer from one division to another meant that two employees would also transfer, in order to provide technical support. The first employee to get there asked his new supervisor what the department was like and whether the associates were friendly. The supervisor asked him if the associates were friendly "back home." "Not particularly," was the reply. "Well," said the supervisor, "I don't think you'll find associates very friendly here, either." When the second man arrived, he also asked the supervisor about the friendliness of the associates, and the supervisor asked him if the associates "back home" were friendly. "Oh, yes!" was his enthusiastic response. "Well," said the supervisor, "you'll find associates here to be very friendly, too!"

The way you view your life's circumstances depends on your attitude. You may choose to see the world around you from a positive or a negative perspective. The way you think and the way you react is totally up to you. Neither your boss, your job, your associates, nor luck creates your attitude. You alone are in control.

Your state of mind plays a major role in your performance on the job, and in your ability to recognize root business problems. Performance and problem-solving involve your mental resources:

your thinking processes, your beliefs, your feelings, and your attitudes toward self, people, events, circumstances, work, and problems. The way you view your business- and job-related problems is a matter of attitude, and your attitude can set you apart from other employees.

A negative or positive attitude will be observed by others in one's behavior, response, and demeanor. Negative attitudes are *destructive* because they tear down one's self-image; a poor self-image, in turn, can damage or destroy meaningful relationships with other people. Stinginess, prejudice, cruelty, distrust, cheating, and corruption are possible results of a negative attitude. On the other hand, positive attitudes are *constructive* because they build up one's self-image; a good self-image, in turn, helps to develop meaningful relationships with other people. Integrity, honesty, generosity, tolerance, kindness, and credibility are possible results of a positive attitude.

Whether destructive or constructive, attitude is a matter of choice — *your* choice. Employers certainly *want* employees who deal with the practical matters of the job, but they *need* employees who have positive attitudes. The movers and shakers of the business world conduct their business affairs by aiming for high goals and constantly striving to achieve them. The state of mind — the positive attitude — that these "be the best" employees have chosen is an ingredient critical to the survival and growth of American business.

All employees would like to be happy and secure, but many haven't understood what they must do to achieve this desire. Specifically, they haven't realized that the main thing that keeps them from getting their wish is their lack of a positive attitude. They haven't experienced job enjoyment, career success, or personal happiness in the past because they haven't learned to expect them. The truth is that these positive experiences are available to everyone.

Attitude: Job Enjoyment

The word "job" seems so limited when, in fact, your job is probably broader than any possible job description. You have direct responsibilities and duties, but I am sure that you find yourself involved in more activities than your narrow job description would indicate. Whatever you consider to be your job, analyze what there is about the job that you like and dislike. Your feelings and beliefs about your job may be difficult to express or describe, but your progress toward better job conditions will be restricted unless you recognize the positives you would like to build upon, and the negatives that you must eliminate. The Job Elements chart on page 76 offers some positive and negative characteristics you may experience with your job today.

If you approach your job determined to minimize the negatives and enjoy the positives, your

JOB ELEMENTS
EXAMPLES

Job Elements	Possible Positive Characteristics	Possible Negative Characteristics
Duties:	Challenging, fun, something new every day	Boring, stressful, unimportant
Associates:	Friendly, helpful, competent	Rude, gossip about me, "they're useless"
Management:	Supportive, interested, communicates	Disinterested, doesn't listen, secretive
Work Environment:	Pleasant, clean	Dirty, disorganized
Customers:	Friendly, courteous	Demanding, unreasonable
Pay Compensation:	Fair, competitive	Ridiculous, "slave wages"
Career Growth:	Helps my goals, a learning experience	Dead-end job, progress is impossible
Personal Development:	Up to me, I must take responsibility	The management ignores my needs

job will be more enjoyable and you will do better work. An active program to strengthen your performance and increase your problem-solving skill leads to success. You have the right to feel good when you are making progress in your business life. A day will come when you consider yourself one of your company's best employees. You will be justifiably proud, and you will discover that doing your best never drains you, but, instead, fills you with self-esteem and self-confidence.

One sure way to have a positive attitude toward your job is to find work that you love to do. Many people hate work simply because they have not found their own place in the scheme of business. Understanding your purpose, knowing how your work helps others, seeing yourself grow as a businessperson, and feeling appreciated all say, "You belong! Others count on you and you need to be there." A sense of joy and excitement comes about when you truly become interested in or enthusiastic about work activities. Enjoyable work should have some of the same characteristics as a favorite college course, a pet project, or a hobby. Just think how productive you could be if your job were as enjoyable as your hobby!

When I was a high school student, a friend invited me to stay after school and join him at his Boy Scout meeting. That particular evening, the troop was offering Morse code practice for those interested in earning a merit badge for communications. As I listened to the instructions for proper copying of the coded messages, something magical happened. I was intrigued with the deciphering process. This simple event aroused my interest in radio communications. Combining my proficiency in copying Morse code with the study of electronic theory soon led to my acquiring an amateur radio license.

My electronics experimentation and design accomplishments became very enjoyable for me. This joy was carried throughout my college and professional career, from designing an automatic animal feed mill system for my dad's farm while I was in college, to designing telecommunication, missile guidance, and process control systems for my employers. The interest and satisfaction gained through a hobby became the basis for job enjoyment in my professional work.

Attitude: Career Success

Your job and career may have come about as the direct result of training for a specific profession, or as the result of a seemingly haphazard sequence of positions and responsibilities. In either case, it is likely that numerous circumstances have led you to the position you currently hold. Whether consciously or subconsciously, you have chosen the paths that got you there. Most likely, you have felt successful if each assignment along the way offered you greater responsibility or

ATTITUDE MANAGEMENT   79

greater financial compensation than the last; however, these visible signs of success are only tem-
poral.

We spend a great deal of effort and money trying to display how successful we are (or wish we
were). Equating success with big cars, new
houses, fur coats, country club memberships, and
the like is missing the truth about success. True
success requires questioning what we really want
out of life, what talents we are willing to use, and
what level of commitment we are prepared to
make to pursue our dreams and goals. It is much
harder to acquire a feeling of inner success than it
is to purchase those things that many think sym-
bolize success.

Success is a very personal thing. In order for
success to be meaningful, you must derive some
satisfaction from it. If an engineer completes a design for a building or a salesman closes a sale,
neither person is successful if he/she finds no satisfaction in doing so. Success must be enjoyed. If
you find no satisfaction, gratification, or enjoyment with your business life, then you haven't acquired the true achievement of success in your
consciousness.

Doing your best to achieve goals is satisfying.
Personal satisfaction comes from knowing that
you have done your best to use your talents fully.
You can enjoy personal success even when job
conditions, projects, and businesses you are involved in appear to have problems or appear to be

failing. It is at those times that it is important to be thinking of how things could be, not how they appear at the moment. Don't settle for second best; instead, choose to reach your potential. Develop the mental attitude that will make your career a success.

Attitude: Personal Happiness

The apparent security offered by material things such as large bank accounts, big homes, or fancy cars will not deliver permanent happiness. Even health, pleasure, and love will not necessarily make one happy. These attributes do not, in themselves, bring happiness. I was asked a tough question by a close friend. The question was simply, "Are you happy?" My first reaction was to say, "No," since I was experiencing confusion, stress, and disappointment at that time. But, as I considered the question more deeply, I learned more about myself and what really makes me happy.

I found that happiness is a state of mind and comes to me through recognition of my own power and the finding of my own place in the world. Likewise, you owe it to yourself to discover what it is you are designed to do as a life-long purpose. Think in terms of a major purpose, then describe it as your MAJOR OBJECTIVE in your life's work. Henry Ford wanted every American family to have an automobile. He created the "assembly line" concept, which produced cars at a price, for the first time, that was affordable by the average American. Personally, my major objective is to increase the world competitiveness of American businesses. To this end, *Working for Success* was created to help America's employees to be more creative, productive, and successful.

A later chapter will help you learn how to find the right role for you in the business world. Once you know what you should be doing, you will feel a little empty until you start to make progress toward your objective. As you achieve intermediate goals, feelings of satisfaction and happiness will fill the void.

Happy employees are contented because they are notably well-adapted or fitted to their work. These employees have unquestioning sureness about their goals, the purpose of their work, and their abilities. For the happy employee, every day is an exciting opportunity to achieve goals and find solutions to tough problems. Happy employees and positive attitudes go hand in hand.

Qualities of the Positive Attitude

The best boss, subordinate, and associate will model a positive attitude. The Qualities of the Positive Attitude chart on page 82 lists some of the key characteristics of a positive attitude. Most

QUALITIES OF THE POSITIVE ATTITUDE

Approachability	Discipline	Inventiveness	Promptness
Attentiveness	Eagerness	Joyousness	Readiness
Caring	Enthusiasm	Kindness	Realism
Cheerfulness	Fairness	Love	Respectfulness
Common Sense	Faithfulness	Loyalty	Sincerity
Compassion	Flexibility	Meekness	Submissiveness
Competitiveness	Friendliness	Motivation	Tactfulness
Consideration	Generosity	Neatness	Teachability
Cooperation	Gentleness	Obedience	Tenacity
Courage	Helpfulness	Open-mindedness	Thoughtfulness
Courtesy	Honesty	Optimism	Tolerance
Credibility	Hopefulness	Organization	Trustworthiness
Dedication	Humbleness	Originality	Understanding
Dependability	Initiative	Passion	Vision
Determination	Integrity	Patience	Willingness

employees don't realize that every person already possesses each of the qualities listed! The magnitude of the quality may be stronger or weaker, depending on the individual's state of personal development, but there is a potential in every person to make these qualities strong. Look at the list, and identify five that you feel are your strong points; then also identity one that you know is weak. Through this self-analysis, you can determine some personal development goals which will move you closer to your major objective, your destiny, your success as one of the best employees.

Wouldn't you prefer to have a boss or employee who possesses a positive attitude? Doesn't it make sense that your employer wants employees who radiate excitement and enthusiasm instead of employees who are lifeless and indifferent? Employees who are caring, joyous, and helpful rather than employees who are jealous, fearful, and worried? Set a goal to change a weak quality into a personal strength, and you, too, can become such a "positive" employee.

What About Adversity?

Even with a positive attitude, you will not be without problems. You cannot always prevent unpleasant circumstances or negative situations from occurring, but you can develop self-control and emotional stability. What happens in your life does not matter as much as how you react to it. For example, if you earn a large sum of money and then lose it due to a calamity, will you have the emotional stability necessary to start all over again?

Merv Griffin of TV game show fame is a celebrated billionaire. His attitude toward this wealth indicates that Mr. Griffin has achieved true success. He says, "Who will care in a hundred years?" When asked what he would do if he lost it all, he said, "I would put a dollar in a glass, sit it on the piano, play and sing for tips as I did when I first started out." A person with a successful frame of mind will set about rebuilding and achieve again. The same business problems that cause one employee to quit his/her job will cause another to strengthen his/her efforts and succeed.

The relationship between an employee and supervisor may produce negative job conditions and, in their minds, real adversity that leads to a disaster. A supervisor assigns projects, problems, and tasks to employees. A supervisor also sets standards of performance, measures the employee's progress, and determines the appropriate compensation. In these and other dealings, many supervisors don't perform their jobs perfectly, and some employees don't accept the authority or judgments of their supervisors willingly. However, each can learn to react to this kind of adversity in a manner that turns a negative condition into a positive performance.

Negative conditions prevailed at one point between my supervisor and me. I worked in a highly interruptive environment. Customer complaints constantly created emergencies that had to be handled immediately. The customer complaint would be channeled to my supervisor first; in turn, he would abruptly interrupt me to press for an explanation. Frequently, I would have to research the facts and get back to my boss immediately with the answers. These interruptions were very stressful, and it was difficult to remain positive because I took the complaints as a personal criticism against me, instead of against our business performance. I was having a hard time handling the unexpected.

One day, a company sent me an "employee goodwill" wall poster sample. The slogan, as best I can remember, stated,

"Management is a series of interruptions, only interrupted by interruptions."

The poster helped me to see that it was my job to handle interruptions. I decided to change my attitude, and with some concentration and practice, I could give my customers and my boss an immediate response without getting ruffled. Those stressful interruptions served a purpose for me and my organization. I learned quickly to spot and solve the root problem that caused the need for the interruption, which helped dramatically to reduce the number of customer complaints and to improve our image as an organization. Through my attitude management, the interruptive environment was eliminated.

Power of Expectations

Many employees feel that most uncertain situations will have unfavorable outcomes. Problems, disappointments, and failures have been occurring all around them, so it is only natural to expect negative conditions. It is likely that you have an acquaintance or two who always look at the pessimistic side of everything. Certainly, you know associates who have very low expectations.

People usually get what they expect. People who expect to find frustration and failure are generally unhappy employees; people who expect to enjoy their jobs are usually successful. An attitude that is characteristic of successful employees is optimism. An optimist expects the best from himself/herself and from others. Optimism gives one the confidence that whatever happens, he/she will make the best of it. A bad day at work will be only a momentary interruption in his/her flow of success. The successful employee will expect things to get better and will act consistently with this thought.

With a positive attitude, you can be continuously motivated under any and all circumstances. You can become a high achiever who enjoys significantly more successes than failures. Most employees are motivated only for a few weeks or a few months. Others maintain their motivation for several years, but a high achiever is motivated for whatever length of time it takes to accomplish his/her goals. This kind of motivation goes uninterrupted because the high achiever stays interested in his/her goal, and is enthusiastic about the daily progress to achieve that goal.

High achievers know that life is a self-fulfilling prophecy. Because successful people expect to succeed, they keep their eyes open to new opportunities. Unhappy individuals don't expect to succeed, so they simply don't see or take advantage of a situation. They think that if they don't expect too much, they won't be disappointed. The high achiever expects the best of himself/herself and others, and knows he/she won't be disappointed.

Importance of Positive Attitude

The importance of a positive attitude escapes the understanding of many employees in American business. Most are preoccupied with the daily chores of the job, and they ignore their inherent mental powers. Too much attention is consumed in the "do what you have to" mode to meet schedules, produce profits, and get results. The previous failures, mistakes, and problems of the organization seem to set the pattern for future results. Clearly, employees with positive attitudes are needed to see beyond the errors of the past and accomplish the goals of the future.

The best employees understand the importance of company objectives. These employees know they have performance and problem-solving abilities that are needed and respected by their employers. Also, these employees know how their positive attitude contributes to the success of the company and to their own success as individuals. But you may not yet see how you can obtain or maintain a positive attitude when your company is not successful, or when your job is stressful, or when your personal career progress is disappointing.

Mental Power Concept

Positive attitude becomes a permanent attribute when you are convinced that your future is under your control. If you really knew that you were in control, wouldn't you have a different view of your current job, of progress with your career, and wouldn't you be happier? The *mental power concept*, when fully understood, will give you the power to control future events in regard to your job, career, and happiness. With control, you can have a positive attitude all the time!

Having GOALS for yourself is essential if you are to develop a positive attitude. Control is only meaningful if you know what it is you want so that you can recognize when you get off course. If you don't have clear goals now, start doing some dreaming and thinking about the things you would like to achieve. Think about your work, your job conditions, and the progress of your career. Can you answer the questions listed in the Personal Career Goals Questionnaire on page 90? Thinking about the questions may help you to recognize how you feel about your job, career, and personal needs; knowing your feelings can lead to the recognition of what you want to be different, better, or more enjoyable. Your feelings can be turned into goals.

When you have clear goals firmly in your mind, all surrounding interruptions, business problems, adversity, failures, and disappointments will have a lesser impact on you as long as you recognize that you are making some progress each day toward the achievement of your goals. If you don't have goals, then your drifting mode of living and working will yield only frustration and unhappiness, and it is likely you won't even realize what is the source of this condition.

The goals you have set for yourself are known only to you. You know what you want to accomplish; you know where you want to go, much like the circus clown walking on stilts through a street crowd. He sees where he is going with his clear view, unlike those individuals in the crowd who have their sight impaired by other people's heads

PERSONAL CAREER GOALS QUESTIONNAIRE

1. What is the most important thing you want to accomplish during your working career years?
2. What's the biggest problem you have to solve this month? This year?
3. What's the most important goal or project you have to achieve this week? This month? This year?
4. What kind of job conditions do you have at this time?
5. What is the level of job performance you are achieving today? Competence? Commitment? Cooperation?
6. Can you recognize the true source of business problems affecting your job and the business of your employer?
7. What kind of attitude and behavior do you demonstrate as you perform your job? Personal character traits?
8. What are the barriers you see today that would interfere with your job enjoyment, career success, and personal happiness?
9. What are the benefits you would like to receive as a result of achieving your goals?
10. What is the timing for you to achieve each goal?
11. What are you willing to commit to in order to achieve your goals?

bobbing up and down. Most of the clown's steps move him forward in the direction he wants to go, but there are times when the crowd brushes against his stilts, resulting in a momentary step backwards. However, he regains his momentum and continues on to reach his desired destination. So will you, if you know where you are going.

With a little practice, you can see how a particular event or experience contributes to your forward progress toward achieving goals. Even little things that happen during the work day may contribute something of value. A word or idea expressed by an associate, a friend, a magazine article, or a television broadcaster may evoke a fresh thought or reinforce your efforts to achieve your goal. Thinking about your goals, or writing them down, or reading them, or doing some pencil planning moves you closer to your goals. Progress may be slow, but there will be progress even if you cannot readily observe it yourself. Some progress manifested each day, no matter how little, indicates that *you will eventually achieve your goal!*

In a later chapter, you will learn how to use your mental powers to identify your goals, think constructively about these goals, develop a more positive attitude, and make positive progress. Professional growth and personal development are impossible without goals, so it is important to take quality time to identify the right goals for you and seek means to achieve these goals in the most effective manner. When you know your goals, then you can do the mental work necessary to seize control of your thinking, behavior, and future. You have the mental power to improve your job performance, increase your problem-solving skills, and manage your attitude to become one of the best!

SECTION II

KNOW THE LAWS

The important natural laws of human endeavor explain the basis for the success of achieving goals. Professional growth and personal development are possible when the laws are understood and applied correctly. *Creativity Laws* provide for the materialization of the job performance, problem solutions, and positive attitude you desire; *Compensation Laws* deliver the enjoyable job conditions, pay, benefits, and resources you desire; and *Growth Laws* govern opportunities, career direction, and progress throughout the years.

CHAPTER 4
Creativity Laws

Art Linkletter tells the story of walking with his friend, Walt Disney, through an orange grove near Anaheim, California. Mr. Disney told Art that he had a dream of building a place there that would give children and families the experience of make-believe and pleasure — a place to enjoy adventure, fantasies, and fun in a wholesome atmosphere. The orange grove was converted into a world-class entertainment center. Walt Disney created a magic kingdom — Disneyland.

The Creativity Laws are concerned with the act of bringing something into being that did not exist before. Because of creativity, raw materials become finished products. For example, a novelist creates a unique view of life by using everyday language; a businessman creates a customer service by employing people; an engineer creates a bridge by preparing drawings; an employee creates more profits by solving a productivity problem. In each case, the Creativity Laws are at work.

The word CREATE also suggests conscious intentions, power, and *control*. Because of desire, ability, and determination, created ideas are materialized into our physical presence. In the laws of the plant kingdom, new plants start from seeds. Whether weeds or flowers, each one has its beginning as a seed. In a similar manner, every human endeavor has its beginning as a seed in the form of thoughts. The natural creativity process starts with the planting of the seed of the things we want to receive and possess. We take control of our destiny when we understand and apply the creativity laws correctly.

The Creativity Laws are Law of Mind, Law of Cause and Effect, and Law of Thought. Through their operations, human achievement and success are created. It is within the framework of these laws that you can use your thinking processes to create the quality of work employers want and the kind of career experience you desire. You possess all you need, right now, to start the creative process.

Source of Creativity

Every human advancement first occurred as an idea, and those ideas took form and became physical reality. Look at the accomplishments of the world's civilizations. Think about the technological progress from inventing the primitive "wheel" to putting a man on the moon and returning him safely! Think of the countless ideas that started in someone's imagination and found their place in history — printing press, cotton gin, steam engine — television, computers, satellite communications, jet aircraft, and nuclear power. Each began as a spark in someone's mind.

Humanity's progress in political, social, and commercial arenas is built upon the countless ideas of leaders and participants in those fields. In the arts, composers and artists illustrate the creative concept of taking an idea — a mental vision — from intangible thoughts to a beautiful melody or picture. In all human endeavors, you will find ideas created by people.

Consider the place where you work. Your employer's business requires countless ideas and plans in order to stay competitive. To grow, the business requires that even more good ideas be executed effectively — ideas which will help to increase sales, reduce costs, improve customer relations, and strengthen the organization. Employers want employees who have these good ideas — who can think creatively — to accomplish the work and solve problems.

Creative Thinking

All around you, you will find expressions of creative ideas of various significance and magnitude. Creative thinking is an activity that leads to new information, or a previously undiscovered solution or condition, rather than to an obvious solution or status quo. Creative thinking is a resource that uses the mental attributes of flexibility, originality, and inventiveness to produce tangible results. Everyone has these abilities at one level or another. Positive-minded people have developed their creative abilities to a level that makes it possible for their dreams to come true.

Being creative doesn't necessarily mean producing something out of thin air. That would be a miracle! But it can mean bringing something into the environment that wasn't present before. An "idea seed" planted can create a new condition in physical reality.

For example, the chairs in our conference room were unattractive and extremely uncomfortable. Our customers, who frequently met with us, were subjected to this discomfort and likely questioned our professionalism. My staff suggested replacing the chairs so that business meetings could be conducted in more comfort, and our professional image could be improved. Two of my staff members agreed to select and purchase the best chairs for the conference room. Three months went by, but no chairs appeared. More pressing business matters occupied the minds of my two staff members.

Then, all of a sudden and without fanfare, eight executive-style, cushioned chairs showed up in the conference room. What's more, they were free. While waiting for my two staff members to complete their commitment, I learned that a remodeling project under way in another division would lead to some surplus furniture. Through a little horse trading, I was able to acquire comfortable and suitable replacement chairs — without spending a dime and by an unexpected channel.

Because the seed had been planted, the environment in our conference room changed. The initial thought had created a desired condition.

If the creative thinking process can change the physical environment at work, why couldn't it produce an improved job performance, discover a problem solution, and develop a positive attitude? As discussed in the chapters of Section I, these characteristics of a "best" employee have their bases in the mental powers of the individual. Competence, commitment, cooperation, problem analysis, and attitude all deal with the mental realm. In fact, using ideas to create desired performance, solutions, and behavior follows a similar thinking process to the one we used to get new chairs, and Walt Disney used to build Disneyland; it only differs by degree. To understand this creative capability better, consider the miracle of a flesh and blood organ called the brain.

The Brain

Your every movement and thought is processed and managed by your brain. There are between 10,000,000,000 and 15,000,000,000 nerve cells in the human cerebral cortex, and these nerve cells are arranged in exact patterns. Newly-developed methods of electro-physiology can draw off currents from these definite cell patterns. Through state-of-the-art electronics, the cell cur-

THE HUMAN BRAIN/
MACHINE COMPUTER SYSTEMS

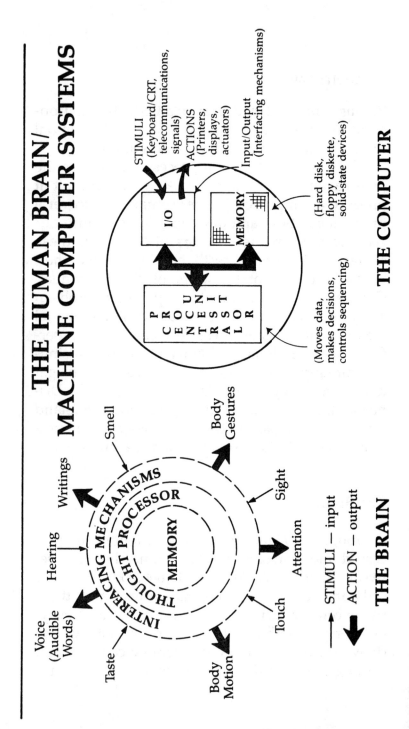

THE COMPUTER

STIMULI
(Keyboard/CRT,
telecommunications,
signals)

ACTIONS
(Printers,
displays,
actuators)

Input/Output
(Interfacing mechanisms)

I/O

MEMORY

(Hard disk,
floppy diskette,
solid-state devices)

PROCESSOR
CONTROL
UNIT

(Moves data,
makes decisions,
controls sequencing)

THE BRAIN

Smell

Body
Gestures

Writings

INTERFACING MECHANISMS

THOUGHT PROCESSOR

MEMORY

Sight

Attention

Hearing

Touch

Voice
(Audible
Words)

Taste

Body
Motion

STIMULI — input
ACTION — output

rents of the brain can be amplified and recorded. These measurements indicate that the brain is an organized machine with the power to control the body and the mind's thinking processes.

Your brain is the equivalent of a trillion-dollar computer between your ears with its ability to make decisions and to store and recall information. This computer works twenty-four hours a day for a lifetime of service. Using the nervous system, the brain responds to the five senses, conducts thinking processes, directs body muscles, and stores experiences — the conscious events that make up an individual life — in its memory. Portable, small, fast, and efficient, its construction is unmatched by any machine invented by man.

Machines use computers as brains — brains that respond automatically to signals, quickly and efficiently performing hundreds of accurate calculations in a split second. Using electrical circuits, computers process information to and from Input/Output devices, store and retrieve data in memory resources, and make logical decisions. Computers can be so complex and sophisticated that they can guide a manned space shuttle into orbit around the earth, send back television pictures of the astronauts, and return the craft accurately to the landing site. But if the engineers program the wrong responses, the computer can't even turn on the cabin heater.

Just as computers are programmed for good results, your brain can erase old beliefs and counter-productive attitudes, and be reprogrammed with new, positive, productive kinds of behavioral conditioning. Why hang onto limiting ideas and beliefs? If you were going to fly to Chicago, and as you got onto the plane the pilot announced that the navigational computer was programmed for Atlanta, wouldn't you want to get off the plane?

You have a fabulous machine you carry around with you every day. It is within your power to train it for the kind of responses that will enable the use of its full capacity. But first, in order to better understand your thinking processes, and to learn how to use your creative capability more consciously, you need to distinguish between the conscious mind and the subconscious mind.

The Two Parts of the Mind

Each individual is equipped with two phases of mind: conscious and subconscious. The conscious is that part of our mind with which we perceive, reason, judge, and accept or reject. Our conscious mind controls the bodily parts and functions that deal with voice, gestures, writings, motion, and attention. Through the conscious mind, we are able to react to sensations of sight, sound, smell, taste, and touch. By the operation of the conscious mind, we are aware of our power to know, to think, to will, and to choose.

The subconscious mind, on the other hand, governs our involuntary reactions and bodily processes. Digestion, circulation, assimilation, and excretion are subconsciously-operated processes. The beating of our hearts and the inflation of our lungs are rote functions, which we do not operate with our conscious mind. The subconscious mind is part of the nervous system, and this complex system works to maintain, rebuild, and operate our bodies.

The subconscious mind is also the seat of habit and instinct, and the storehouse of memory. All of life's experiences are stored away in our memory bank ready for our use. The subconscious mind provides the source for emotional and impulsive behavior, feelings, beliefs, attitude, character traits, and wisdom. It is these important characteristics that make up the personality which is observable by one's associates, superiors, and customers.

The subconscious mind does not reason or judge. This portion of our mental powers cannot reject because it *always* accepts. The subconscious accepts all thoughts and suggestions supplied by the conscious mind, whether they are true or false, fact or fiction, positive or negative, good or evil. The subconscious mind will accept thoughts and suggestions as a pattern to work for as it sets

THE HUMAN MIND IN COMPUTER TERMS

The Physical World

STIMULI

Sight
Taste
Smell
Touch
Hearing

ACTIONS

Voice
Gestures
Writings
Motion
Attention

The Mental World

Imagination & Ideas

I/O

Thought Processor

- Knowledge
- Emotions
- Habits
- Instincts
- Character
- Values

- Beliefs
- Choices
- Behavior
- Awareness
- Attitudes
- Feelings

Conscious Mind

MEMORY

INFORMATION

Subconscious Mind

THE BRAIN

about acquiring our conscious desires. The conscious mind is the *supreme ruler* of the subconscious mind!

The conscious mind and the subconscious mind work together to process stimuli, information, and decisions. Some thinking will appear to be automatic, which is a response according to training and conditioning of the subconscious mind. Other learned responses will be intentionally programmed because the attention of the conscious mind has been directed to concentrate, thereby penetrating straight to the subconscious mind. The conscious mind deals with the realm of physical awareness while the subconscious mind deals with the realm of internal thoughts.

Imagination

The subconscious mind doesn't know the difference between a real and imagined experience — only the conscious mind can reason and judge. Therefore, it follows that imaginary experiences are just as much a conditioner of attitudes, responses, and habits as real experiences! A person can condition himself/herself to success responses by using his/her imagination to create a success experience in his/her mind.

Do you want to demonstrate better job performance, find answers to your problems, and achieve success? Then build it in your imagination. It must first be in your mind before it will ever be anywhere else. Don't stop to think about all the reasons that you shouldn't or couldn't achieve your goal. Don't be concerned about the channel by which you will receive the benefits you desire. Make a clear mental picture of the conditions you want, and hold it in your mind as your own. The visualization of your goal impresses a pattern for your subconscious mind to work for to mold your future.

Creative Power

The subconscious mind works tirelessly and without question. It can give you a new state of mind by breaking old habits, changing distorted beliefs, and building attractive character traits. Just by directing your conscious thoughts (awareness of ideas and desires conceived in the conscious mind) through to your subconscious mind, you can create new "success" attitude-habits and behavior-habits — you can create the person you desire to be. You have the power to take the raw material of "thought" to create your new self in preparation for enormous success.

Beliefs held by the subconscious mind tend to be in harmony with the conditions surrounding the individual. If one thinks that a goal is impossible to achieve, the subconscious mind gives up on that goal, thereby confirming that success is beyond reach. On the other hand, if the belief acknowledged by the conscious mind is affirmative, the subconscious mind will influence the individual's actions to bring about achievement of the goal. Only if the individual's subconscious mind is brought into harmony with the idea of the goal will the object of the goal materialize. The inner self will not be at rest until the external conditions the subconscious mind is working for are achieved. This materialization process is stated by the Law of Mind.

Law of Mind: YOUR SUBCONSCIOUS MIND
WORKS TO MATERIALIZE ANY
IDEA OR BELIEF SUPPLIED BY
YOUR CONSCIOUS MIND.

When the imagination is used to visualize a goal, conscious thoughts about the goal are impressed upon the subconscious mind. The goal is the idea desired. Whether your goal is to improve job performance, solve a tough problem, or improve a personal character quality, the subconscious mind is waiting for direction. If you "believe" you will achieve the benefits of enjoyable job conditions, career success, and personal happiness, your subconscious mind will work to bring this success to you. These wishes can be goals, too. Remember, the subconscious mind doesn't acknowledge limitations or lacks — it accepts ideas and beliefs that you consciously set as goals.

Unseen Causes; Tangible Effects

We live and work in a "cause and effect" world. Every event of human origin is first worked out in the unseen idea realm before it appears in tangible form. The realm of the unseen is the realm of cause; the realm of the seen is the realm of effect. All that was ever accomplished in the business world was first conceived in someone's mind. Every diagnosis originated in the mind of a doctor, every computer program originated in the mind of a programmer, and every building originated in the mind of an architect. Ideas and thoughts worked out in the mind cause objects to be manifested in our environment.

In a similar manner, undesirable performance and behavior have their beginnings in the mind of the employee. The cause for this destructive result lies in the private and unseen thoughts of the employee. The internal thoughts that impress the subconscious mind can be intentionally created by the individual, but there is another source of suggestions. Nothing is missed by your five senses even when you may not be aware of information being absorbed by your subconscious mind. Subliminal impressions on the subconscious mind can occur without being perceived by the conscious mind.

For example, the 1957 movie *Picnic* interwove frames into the film that had message images saying, "Eat popcorn," and "Drink Coca-Cola." Even though the messages were on the screen for approximately one thousandth of a second, popcorn sales increased by 58%, and Coke sales increased by 18%. This technique was outlawed by the federal government because the viewers were moved to buy products without detecting the presence of the suggestion. The images of the messages were detected by the eyes which, in turn, caused the idea (thought), which resulted in the action of purchasing food.

In the case of this movie, the messages were repeated many times. Each person in the audience reacted to the messages consistent with their state of mind and personal development. Repetition of any suggestion tends to produce ideas or reinforce beliefs already held. The relationship between subconscious thought patterns conducted in the unseen realm and the behavior observed in the visible realm is controlled by the Law of Cause and Effect.

Law of Cause and Effect: FOR YOUR EVERY
                                            THOUGHT THERE IS
                                            A RESULT.

Beliefs, feelings, and attitudes are *built* of the countless thoughts permitted to be presented to the subconscious mind. In fact, each idea and thought, as well as each picture seen and word heard, will influence beliefs, feelings, and attitudes which lead to behavior. The magnitude of the outcome will be proportionate to the intensity and repetition of the thought. Years of thinking ethical and moral thoughts will have their result: positive character which leads to success. On the other hand, years of thinking unethical and immoral thoughts will also have their result: negative character which leads to failure. So, be on guard. Be careful and watchful of the kind of thoughts that occupy your mind.

This law has a significant impact on your business life. Employees who make a public display of anger toward the boss or another associate probably are not aware of what is really happening to them. They fail to see that they have allowed themselves to be conditioned for this kind of behavior. Either intentionally or unintentionally, they have permitted negative emotions (information) to be stored in their memory. Their angry emotions or rash impulses are caused by the cumulation of experiences and thinking patterns. The Law of Cause and Effect can work for good or for bad. You can choose, through conscious effort, to reject destructive, negative thoughts. Let your predominant thoughts be positive ones.

Predominant Thought

The things you think about frequently and the topics your mind dwells upon constantly make up the predominant thought of your consciousness. Topics may be positive (as in wishing for a successful project) or negative (as in complaining about job stress). Walt Disney's predominant thought was to see his dream of Disneyland come true. His reputation, life savings, and business became committed because of his mental vision and preoccupation with seeing it built. Whatever topic your conscious mind holds as the most important will have the highest priority for your attention. This predominant thought starts a chain of events that leads to the manifestation of this thought into conditions.

The results of your predominant thought are the conditions you truly desire to see fulfilled. The job performance you demonstrate, your effectiveness in solving root business problems, and your mental attitude are representative of your thinking. The relationships you have with people and the quality of the work you do are representative of your thinking. Acquiring enjoyable job conditions, career success, and personal happiness are results that are representative of your thinking. Predominant thought is thinking that leads to conditions desired; simply stated it is the Law of Thought.

> *Law of Thought:* YOUR PREDOMINANT
> THOUGHT CREATES DESIRED
> CONDITIONS.

Reflect on your thoughts about your job, your company, and the people with whom you come into contact. Perhaps a difficult business situation

occurred at some point in your career. Perhaps
you were laid off from a job, or you were overlooked for a promotion, or failed to complete a
project on time, or experienced conflict with an
associate. Ask yourself how your attitudes at the
time affected your situation. If you held negative
thoughts regarding the situation and could visualize no positive resolution, no happy ending, then,
undoubtedly, none occurred. Whatever thoughts
you allowed to preoccupy your mind became your
belief, or, your "faith." You believed so intently in
the negative outcome that your conviction held!
Perhaps, on the other hand, you acted with hope
of finding better conditions. You found a better
position or project assignment. Believing in positive outcomes increases the likelihood that positive results will occur.

*We are all creating our own lives from within our
own minds.* Visible conditions of one's job and life
are simply the outward manifestations of the
inner self. Income, daily responsibilities, and
place in the hierarchy of the company have been
determined by one's thinking. For example,
the employee whose predominant thought is
PROMOTION to a manager's position will think
like a manager while performing his/her current
assignment. The day will come when, by some
channel, success will come to this employee. But
if an employee thinks about nothing but escape
from the job, he/she will eventually see this wish

come true, and maybe not by choice! In each case, the employee's mind created the outcome: his/her world.

Your Mind Development

Both creative and unimaginative thinkers frequently work within the same office walls but are as far apart as their thought processes. Yet both may choose to blame their failures on others or on bad luck. However, an individual's failure lies not in others or in misguided luck, but in his/her own thinking. What people fail to see is that their ability to guide their success is within their own mind.

Mind development is the key to creative accomplishments. Being of good character, having clever ideas, being quick to solve problems, and having a good memory represent a few of the positive characteristics of a person using more than ten percent of his/her mental powers. How did you develop your mind? What is the source of your attitudes? I offer the suggestion that your present character and attitudes are made up of countless sensory impressions, thoughts, and habits entertained and formed by YOU in the past. Your personality primarily results from your cumulative experience, starting in childhood. Researchers estimate that by the time a person reaches adulthood, he/she will have been exposed to the word "no" and other negative suggestions 40,000 times. These experiences produce ideas of limit and lack, and can cause a child to develop a poor self-image.

As with an adult, every thought that enters a child's mind and every situation or event that touches a child's life will plant a seed in that child's subconscious because the subconscious accepts all stimuli, both positive and negative. A child's subconscious is more sensitive than an adult's to the suggestions and ideas of others, because the child's conscious mind isn't fully developed to reject or judge. When a person grows up with so many suggestions of limit and lack, change can only happen when his/her mind is reconditioned with ideas of success. Childhood experience is the basis for all future action unless the person SYSTEMATICALLY SETS ABOUT CHANGING HIS/HER PREDOMINANT THOUGHT.

Constructive Thinking

To think constructively is to concentrate with a definite purpose and technique in order to achieve a specific goal. It is concentration that channels your predominant (conscious) thought of your desires into your subconscious mind. Creation of plans, creation of problem solutions, and finding answers to important questions are possible through such concentration, and new character traits can also be built in this way.

In order to better understand your creative capability, stop for a minute and just sit quietly. You will become aware of what you are thinking, whether in the form of words, images, or flashes of ideas. For an experiment, pick just one thought or subject you like; then think and reflect upon this topic — and nothing else — for one minute. This event will be either fun or real work depending on your present state of mind and the development of your thinking processes. *If you tried the experiment, you have experienced the mental work that starts the creative process.* Your thoughts are "things" themselves — raw materials that can be formed by you and converted into the conditions you desire. The chain of events leading to success is set into motion by you.

The more effort you exert in the process of developing your mental powers, the more creativity you will attain. The Creativity Laws show that thought is a creative force you can use to control your performance, attitude, and behavior, as a prerequisite to controlling your future success. In a later chapter, you will learn how to change or re-direct your day-to-day thoughts so that you can create the success you have been looking for!

CHAPTER 5
Compensation Laws

Lee Iacocca worked up through the ranks of Ford Motor Company to become its president. Years later, he left Ford and became Chrysler's president when Chrysler was near bankruptcy. Mr. Iacocca started his job at Chrysler without taking a salary. In record time, he brought Chrysler back from the brink of financial disaster to financial well-being — even repaying its $1.2 billion government loan before it was due! The Board of Directors now pays him an annual salary in the millions. Chrysler's stockholders, whose investments were at risk, believe Mr. Iacocca's compensation is worth every penny.

In addition to being a successful businessman, Lee Iacocca became a media celebrity, newsmaker, and a man many urged to run for President of the United States. Pay, fame, and personal satisfaction all became the compensation for this business-man. Clearly, his state of professional growth and personal development is being compensated. This compensation is made possible by the Compensation Laws.

Compensation means payment or remuneration for a service, kindness, or benefit given to another person or persons — an age-old system of doing something for someone else and then getting something back of equal value. Salary and benefits are compensation, but compensation can encompass a great deal more than a paycheck. Enjoyable work, challenge, advancement opportunity, and recognition are conditions that usually enhance the value of financial compensation. Achievement of goals we set for ouselves can be the most satisfying compensation.

The Compensation Laws are the Law of Recompense and the Law of Attraction. These laws deal with giving and receiving, sowing and reaping. It is within these laws that we learn of the natural process of sowing a thought in the subconscious mind and reaping a goal in the conscious world. Our goal — to achieve enjoyable job conditions, fair pay, desired benefits and resources — is made possible by the Compensation Laws.

Consistency of Nature

Nature does not allow us to sow seeds of one kind and reap fruits of another. If you plant corn seeds in your garden, there is no doubt they will produce no other crop than corn. If you plant bluegrass seeds in your new yard, you will be mowing bluegrass, not rye, next spring. Nature does not make mistakes; the crop is always consistent with the kind of seed planted. Each seed will develop the kind, form, and characteristics of its own nature because the unseen patterns of each must be followed.

The unseen patterns of nature's product also determine the quality of the final product. Corn seed is available in various grades, and there are different hybrids that will have specific growth characteristics. Bluegrass seed quality is based upon the degree to which pure bluegrass predominates over the inevitable presence of foreign grass and weed seeds. In both corn and bluegrass, the peculiar qualities of each seed are brought forth consistently by nature.

Our thoughts are similar to seeds. We cannot sow thoughts of one kind and reap conditions of another. Every time a predominant thought is entertained by us, a chain of action is set into motion which produces attitudes and behaviors consistent with the kind and quality of the thought. We sow actions consistent with our attitudes and behaviors. We reap conditions consistent with our actions. The results are predictable; they work within the Law of Recompense.

Law of Recompense: YOU REAP WHAT YOU SOW IN
　　　　　　　　　BOTH KIND AND QUALITY
　　　　　　　　　WITH EXACT PRECISION.

As with any law, the Law of Recompense will not have results that are random or haphazard. To sow a "thought seed" in our subconscious is a process similar to sowing a seed in the soil. In both cases, manifestation of the seed will be the natural outcome. If you are consumed with thoughts that are anxious, envious, fearful, or hateful, you will emit negative attitudes and reap negative conditions. For example, trying to gain a position in your organization by wishing harm or failure to an associate currently holding the job will eventually bring you frustration and failure — guaranteed!

On the other hand, if you consistently think in terms of success for this associate, then you cannot reap defeat and failure. Your inner thoughts will shape your attitude and behavior toward this associate; this state of mind will be evident by your talk, gestures, and willingness to help. These actions will be recognized by the associate, other associates, and superiors. Employees with a high level of cooperation are desired by employers. Your willingness to help another to be successful will reap success for you.

Sow A Thought — Reap A Condition

Our imaginations can be used to sow thoughts into our subconscious mind; we don't have to rely only on what the five senses can observe or detect. The world we see with our conscious mind may not be the world we want to create for ourselves. Using our power to visualize, we can create the ideas and thoughts that describe the conditions we do want. Whether we want better interpersonal relationships with others, or better job conditions, or to accomplish a goal, we can imagine it first in our minds with the "Sow a Thought" System (see page 122).

Your subconscious mind will accept all suggestions as patterns to work for. Under your conscious control, you can override past negative programming by replacing it with conscious, positive new directions. This is accomplished through "self-talk" — the act of consciously thinking of desired conditions and presenting thoughts of these conditions to your subconscious mind. Talking to yourself either mentally or audibly causes imagined conditions to be programmed into the subconscious. Whether your talk is positive or negative, constructive or destructive, good or evil, what you say affirms what you want to believe to be true.

You can make up any self-talk affirmation appropriate for the situation. For example, an affirmation such as, "I will accomplish my goal by January," impresses your subconscious mind with the determination and desire to achieve this condition. If your goal is to become a more friendly person, you might say to yourself, "I am a good listener. I show interest in other people." Your subconscious will work to actually become the new character you are building. You will reap desired conditions consistent with your beliefs.

"SOW A THOUGHT" SYSTEM

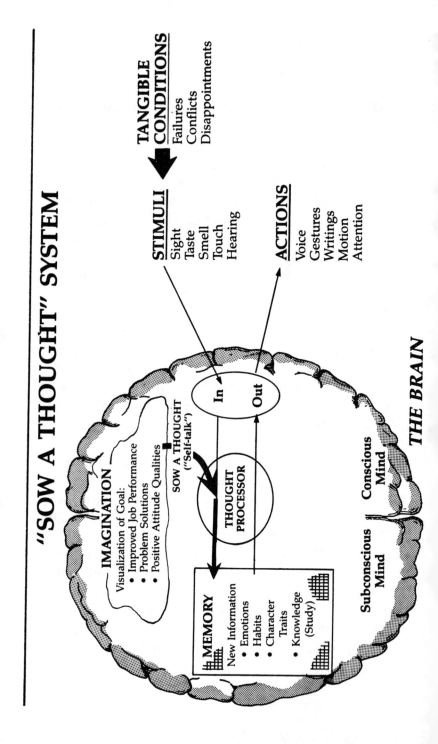

TANGIBLE CONDITIONS
Failures
Conflicts
Disappointments

STIMULI
Sight
Taste
Smell
Touch
Hearing

ACTIONS
Voice
Gestures
Writings
Motion
Attention

IMAGINATION
Visualization of Goal:
• Improved Job Performance
• Problem Solutions
• Positive Attitude Qualities

SOW A THOUGHT
("Self-talk")

In
Out

THOUGHT PROCESSOR

MEMORY
New Information
• Emotions
• Habits
• Character Traits
• Knowledge (Study)

Subconscious Mind

Conscious Mind

THE BRAIN

What you say to yourself and to others will guide your accomplishments and success. Programming of the subconscious mind creates beliefs, beliefs create attitudes, attitudes create feelings that produce action, and actions create results — conditions of improved job performance, problem solutions, and positive attitude made possible by the "Reap a Condition" System (see page 124). Imagining you have successfully achieved one of your goals will convince your subconscious mind, which will convince your body, and you will start to look, breathe, walk, and act like a success. When you master this mental skill, you will accomplish more and enjoy more success. Soon, you will be recognized as one of the "best" employees.

Success Habits

We are "creatures of habit" in both mind and body. Our job conditions, our lives, our careers show accurately what we habitually think. Our character is the result of our thinking, too. "Character" can be defined as the peculiar qualities impressed by natural "gifts" and developed habits, which separate the person possessing them from all others. Thus, we find that each person is the product of his/her own prevailing habits of thought, and by the Compensation Laws, our

"REAP A CONDITION" SYSTEM

STIMULI

Sight
Taste
Smell
Touch
Hearing

ACTIONS

Voice
Gestures
Writings
Motion
Attention

REAP CONDITIONS

Improved Job
Performance
Problem Solutions
Positive Attitude

In

Out

THOUGHT PROCESSOR

New Consciousness
(Belief Goals can be accomplished)

Conscious Mind

Success Habits

MEMORY

New
Conditioning
• Emotions
• Habits
• Character
  Traits
• Knowledge
  (Study)

Subconscious Mind

THE BRAIN

personalities and surrounding conditions reflect what we inherently are.

It has been said, "Sow a thought and reap a character; sow a character and reap an action; sow an action and reap a destiny." Your destiny starts with and is determined by your predominant thought habits. In the final analysis, your place in the business world will be in harmony with and consistent with your mental images, thinking patterns, and personal character. These attributes are formed by the kind and quality of thoughts habitually entertained in your mind.

We all know that habits are hard to break, so when you start to change your old thinking habits, you must be on guard because in the beginning everything may seem to go against you. When you first learned to parallel park your car, you undoubtedly had to try several times until you were able to gain the skill. If you didn't give up, the thought process necessary to parallel park became a successful habit — a skill that you don't have to think about, acquired by frequent repetition. Attitude- and behavior-habits work in the same manner; you must keep trying if you are to develop a new mental skill.

Attraction Power

What we radiate in our thoughts, attitudes, and behavior, we attract into our life and business affairs. It is our predominant thought that can build attractive character, inspire creative ideas, and govern wise choices. This successful behavior can produce job accomplishments that will tend to attract people, resources, and favorable circumstances as compensation for our mental work. From our inner thoughts, we display actions that attract conditions we earn.

Like a magnet with its negative and positive polarity, we draw to ourselves those negative or positive conditions with which we are in harmony. Just as a magnet attracts metallic objects, our thoughts will attract the physical manifestion of the image held in our minds. This relationship is expressed by the Law of Attraction.

Law of Attraction: LIKES ATTRACT.

Although this fundamental law is expressed in simple terms, it represents real power. Thoughts about your goals work under this law. Whatever you set as a goal is possible when you fully understand the natural laws of human endeavor. A new job, a job promotion, or a successful project can be yours if you develop an image of it and concentrate on that image. Hold it in your mind and believe in it with all your strength. See its image vividly and in great detail. Through your complete concentration, a way to achieve the goal will present itself.

As you concentrate on your goal, your thought attracts many thoughts and ideas that you have encountered before or that are similar to the original thought. At other times, new ideas relating to your goal may pop into your head at just the right moment. When you choose to take action on one of these ideas, the manifestation of your goal will become more attainable. When you continue this concentration and action process, the desired condition will in time be yours. Your compensation will be the accomplishment of your goal — LIKES ATTRACT!

Want More Money?

In Chapter 1, I told Jim that his compensation today and in the future will be equivalent to the state of his professional growth and personal development. When Jim looked annoyed with this, I was sure he was thinking about compensation in terms of cash while I was thinking about the "idea of money." Our society has often seemed to be divided between those who believe money is more important than accomplishment and those who believe accomplishment is more important than money. However, financial compensation is based in the idea that they are the same — money is accomplishment, accomplishment is money.

Money can be easily and simply defined as a medium of exchange that is generally accepted as such by the public. It is anything that we are willing to accept from others in return for giving up to them "items" we possess, and that, in turn, other people are willing to accept in return for the items that they give up to us. The "idea of money" is a concept of measuring and expressing relative values of different goods and services.

What gives money value? Contrary to popular belief, the value per unit of our present money supply is independent of any gold or silver backing! The value of money is what money will buy; that is, what it is worth as a medium of exchange. The important point for us to understand as employees is that our employer equates money to the kind and quality of services provided by his/her work force. Payroll and fringe benefits are mediums of exchange for the value of services given: individual accomplishments that contribute to the employer's success.

The only way to earn more money, and to be able to enjoy it, is to come up with ideas (i.e., goods and services) worth money. The ease with which you can do this is made possible by your mental capacity, which is a consciousness defined by your state of professional growth and personal development. It is these characteristics that distinguish you as a personality. Thus, accomplishments produced by your mental capacity will be compensated, and, therefore, your money is an extension of your personality. The more positive your personality, the more money you will attract, and the more you'll enjoy that money. In the long run, you will reap financial benefits in proportion to your personality.

Interpersonal Relationships

People are magnets; but people don't attract "things," they attract other people. "Other people" control money, resources, and opportunities. The job conditions and work environment you seek for yourself are possible when other people give you support, encouragement, and cooperation. If your goal is to close on a big sale, the department secretary who types and mails the proposal helps to make the sale possible. Or, if your goal is to complete a project on time, the associates who contribute their help make the project a success. You must attract people to help you if you are to achieve your goals.

The Law of Attraction can in one sense express the relationship that exists between two individuals. The Interpersonal Communications System illustration on page 130 shows a relationship in which the behavior of one person is observed by another. Simultaneously, the second person is radiating a behavior that is observed by the first. The prevailing thoughts and the automatic responses stored in the subconscious mind are responsible for attraction or rejection of a healthy relationship between these two personalities.

"INTERPERSONAL COMMUNICATIONS" SYSTEM

Sphere of Influence

PERSONALITY "A"

Thoughts
Beliefs
Attitudes
Feelings

Recognition

Behavior

In

Out

STIMULI

Sight
Taste
Smell
Touch
Hearing

ACTIONS

Voice
Gestures
Writings
Motion
Attention

PERSONALITY "B"

In

Out

Recognition

Behavior

Thoughts
Beliefs
Attitudes
Feelings

You are likely to be attracted to people who have similar attitudes toward work, their company, and outside interests. On the other hand, you may know people with whom you don't share a common attitude. It is likely you will work together with them as dictated by the job, but avoid social time together. The likelihood is great that two people with the same kind and quality of thoughts, beliefs, and attitudes will be attracted to each other. In fact, it is inevitable because it is in accord with the Law of Attraction.

Opportunity Magnet

In order to attract the people who control money, resources, and opportunities, it is necessary to move yourself from where you are today to where they are. Remember, a magnet cannot attract a metal object if it is not in range of the object. You have to get close enough to exert some influence on the people you want to attract. For positive results, *your objective should be to achieve your goal while giving something of equivalent value in return.*

There are many people already in your sphere of influence. Your sphere of influence can be expanded to include new relationships that represent sources where new opportunities might be discovered. Everyone with whom you come in contact represents a potential opportunity to ex-

SPHERE OF INFLUENCE

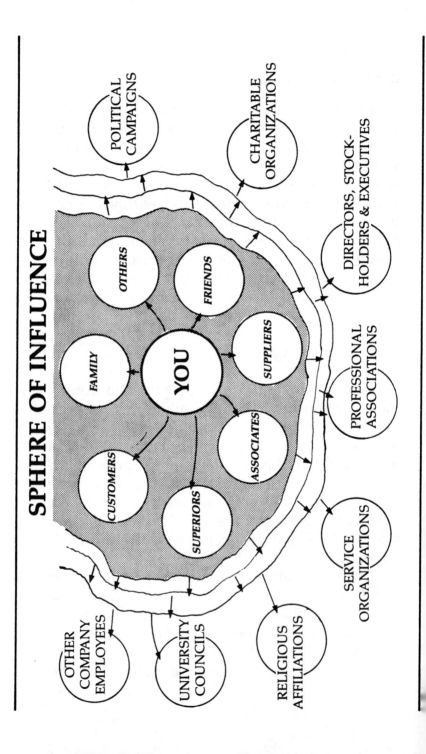

change help and support. You should look for the people who have the best opportunities. You can tell who they are because they are the "best" people. Learn to attract them, and you will become a magnet for opportunity.

If you have a clerical job and you spend your breaks and some personal time with the other clerks in your department, you will have an opportunity to build personal relationships, but you are not likely to attract an opportunity for a promotion in one of the company's other divisions. On the other hand, if you volunteer to lead the company's United Way drive, or serve on the Safety Committee, or author an article in the company newsletter, you may have an opportunity to be exposed to company decision-makers. These leadership opportunities may not be available to you at this time, but the point is that you must be ready to move out of your "comfortable" environment when the time comes if you want the opportunity to influence and attract new people.

As you make contacts and meet new people, you won't find opportunities that can bring you better conditions just sitting in plain view. First, you must know what it is you are looking for. Know your goals, and discover the actions necessary to achieve them. Then, see people and be interested in what they have to say. Look for needs that you can fill. Helping others will help you move closer to your goal.

For example, if you learn that the department manager needs assistance to gather information or to address a customer complaint, don't hesitate to volunteer your help. It may not be your job or responsibility, but you may be in a position to provide a valuable service. Be on the lookout for circumstances where you can contribute support or solutions. Employers want employees who extend themselves to accomplish work; helping another associate or superior is a contribution worthy of recognition.

Relationships Leading To Success

Your relationships with people will play a significant role in your efforts to enjoy your job and to build a successful career. You attract career opportunities by attracting those people who can create jobs, control growth, or provide introductions to others. Your thoughts need to be of the kind and quality that attract positive-minded people.

Positive people want the absolute best for themselves and for others. They are happy when you succeed and hope that your efforts will lead to your happiness. These men and women honestly hope your ideas and plans will be accepted; they hope you will be a positive contributor to the company; and they hope you will get good promotions. They rejoice in your success!

Negative people don't want your life to be any better than theirs. Again, likes attract. These people tend to wish you the same "bad luck" they have, or worse, primarily because of jealousy or envy. They want you to be satisfied with a low salary and an entry-level position. They want you to be content with your conditions, and they make no effort to assist you. They do not want you to get ahead because that would leave them further behind.

It is difficult to separate yourself from these negative personalities, but your disassociation from their negativism is imperative. The negative thoughts expressed by these people will find a place in your mind. And if you express negative thoughts in your conversations, your own ears bring them back to you and reinforce the wrong ideas in your subconscious mind. Therefore, begin to examine your business companions. Associate with optimistic and positive-minded people.

Avoid Negative Results

Cultivate the habit of thinking positive thoughts about yourself and others. If you have failed at a task, put it behind you and start thinking "success." Replace your unhappy thoughts with happy images. If you think of discordant conditions, more such conditions will manifest themselves in your life. However, since likes attract, the more you think positively, the more you will reap positive conditions.

You may have heard of the Failure Complex through which some people systematically fail. This is the application of the negative side of the Law of Attraction. People who consistently fail are driven by the negative power of their thoughts. They attract the things they fear or the subject of their predominant subconscious impressions. An acquaintance of mine started up several businesses that ended in failure. Each time he failed, the impression of failure grew greater. While he gave his time to each venture, his heart was not in his work. His father was a successful entrepreneur, but the son was mechanically inclined and he really wanted to use his hands to build custom cars instead of running a business. He had subconsciously desired to be rid of his work, and events had shaped themselves in accord with his mental demand. He attracted negative results.

An employee who is consumed by fear and worry will not be the best performer because he/she will radiate these inner feelings, which will be observed by associates, superiors, and customers. Being recognized as a "problem" employee will lead to another failure. By contrast, employees who concentrate on achieving positive results and whose attitudes reflect their hope and determination are the ones who continually succeed.

For many years, I played once a week in our company's golf league. The course we played had a water hazard right in front of the first tee. Many times I walked up to the tee eyeing the hazard, placed the ball on the tee, and straight away drove the ball right into the water. I let myself think of the ball going into the water instead of landing in the fairway as a perfect 220-yard drive. My mental and physical skills weren't very well developed. Clearly, the professional golfers on the PGA tour have mastered these skills of visualization, concentration, and body coordination.

We understand the necessity for athletes to concentrate, exercise, and practice. But we may not understand that our state of professional growth and personal development can benefit from the same process. Working at our jobs will take the same effort a professional golfer exerts if we are to enjoy enormous success on our jobs and in our business careers. Every day is an opportunity to sharpen our business skills, practice mental skills, and be a "pro."

Timing For Compensation

Many people distrust the idea that positive thinking and concentrating on goals will work for them, since they don't see immediate results. It is unfortunate that television has taught us that a complex mystery can be solved in only sixty minutes. Real-life developments do take time; anything worthwhile in life takes time. Just as it takes time for an acorn to grow into a mighty oak tree, your professional growth and personal development will take time to mature into full bloom. Whether you choose to acknowledge the existence of law or not, you will eventually "be" what you predominantly think about; and you will "get" that which you think about, with exact precision.

Everything in our Universe will seek equilibrium. You can get your car up to 60 miles per hour by using the combustion power of the engine combined with the mechanical leverage of the drive train, but just as soon as you run out of gas, the car will come to a stop. The car is always in equilibrium with the force applied. In a similar manner, your actions are always in equilibrium with the kind and quality of your predominant thought. Your predominant thought moves you from a motionless state to an active state which, in turn, attracts equivalent conditions to maintain equilibrium. Whether good or bad, positive or negative, outward conditions will seek equilibrium — compensation matching the originating predominant thought seed.

Your subconscious cannot distinguish between tangible facts and imagined facts. This means if you present imagined desires strongly enough and vividly enough, they will be accepted as real! Therefore, cultivate in yourself courage, determination, enthusiasm, ambition, desire for good, and faith in yourself. Add to these indispensable attributes love for your fellow man and faith in

the ultimate good of all things. With this kind
and quality of positive thinking, your mental attitude will attract equivalent conditions for yourself.

Lee Iacocca received compensation for his service to Chrysler stockholders and employees. The
business turn-around for Chrysler did not happen
by chance, or because Mr. Iacocca is lucky. His
personality shows through even in his TV adver-
tisements. Lee Iacocca earned his financial pay,
fame, and satisfaction (personal satisfaction is enjoying true success) by using his mental capacity;
his state of professional growth and personal development was equal to the task!

CHAPTER 6
Growth Laws

Glen Campbell is a celebrated entertainer. His talents include being an accomplished guitar artist, singer, and television and movie actor. This youthful-looking personality seems comfortable and confident while performing in front of both cameras and live audiences. To many, Mr. Campbell may have appeared to be an internationally famous "overnight success."

Like many young hopefuls, Glen Campbell dreamed of being a "star" in Hollywood's traditional terms. He took his guitar to Hollywood and got involved in the entertainment industry. Mr. Campbell worked as a backup artist in music recording studios. Playing guitar and singing harmony, he continued to develop his musical talents and personality. In fact, he worked behind the scenes at his chosen career nearly ten years before he was in the limelight. Glen Campbell's state of professional growth and personal development evolved from his desire; his career blossomed with each opportunity to perform.

Growth and development is a process of increase and expansion until maturity is reached. All living things experience this building process. A baby becomes an adolescent and then an adult. A high school student becomes a college freshman and then an alumnus. A trainee becomes an associate, then a contributing professional. To achieve one's full potential is to reap the mature fruits of a life-long career.

The Growth Laws are the Law of Opportunity Supply and the Law of Increase. These laws deal with the process of building dreams into reality. It is within these laws that we can learn how supply and demand find equilibrium in the workplace. Continued expansion of our mental capacity prepares us for larger and more satisfying experiences, which are possible by capitalizing on the opportunities surrounding us.

Growth Starts With A Seed

In the vegetable kingdom, a seed is nurtured and transformed by the soil, moisture, and sun until the resulting plant can bear mature fruit. With deep roots, the plant can withstand wind and weeds. In a similar manner, our predominant thoughts can grow and be realized if they are protected from the wind and weeds of life. They need to withstand the criticisms of others and our own lack of purpose. We must nurture our thoughts until they reach full potential.

Your professional growth and personal development start with your thoughts. Your thoughts are the raw material, and your thinking processes supply the energy. It is this combination of raw materials and energy which can plant an idea seed that when nurtured and strengthened creates a demand on the opportunity supply.

The opportunity supply comes from people who control money, resources, and opportunities, and who are helpful and supportive. An opportunity can range from a cordial smile all the way to the creation of a new job that is perfect for you at the moment. Opportunity supply can come in small doses that may just offer you encouragement, or large doses that offer a career-building challenge. The opportunity to improve your job conditions may come from an unexpected channel such as the cooperative support of an associate assigned to your project. It is people who provide opportunity supply; opportunity supply is available in abundance.

Abundance

Abundance is the natural law of the universe. All around us nature is lavish and bountiful. Every seed that grows multiplies fifty times and those fifty bring forth a hundred and those hundred bring forth a thousand. The only limit experienced in this growing process is the result of someone's conscious intentions to withhold or alter the rain and sunshine patterns. Nature knows no other outcome but abundance!

Our national economy has its basis in the vast natural resources found in America. The abundance of land, water, timber, petroleum, natural gas, farm lands, minerals, and other natural materials has set us apart from most other countries in the world. With the rising demand for goods and services by consumers and government agencies, the raw materials from our natural resources are moved, stored, processed, and replaced. The need to convert raw materials into finished products and distribute these products to customers creates the demand for employees who will continue this process. Jobs and careers are created or eliminated as our economy, business, and markets continually change.

These changes are evidenced by the trends in America's economy. For example, we know that America has shifted from an industrial society to a society that is based on the creation and distribution of information. It is the age of computers. Another significant trend is that Americans are now choosing to live in the South and West rather than the old industrial cities of the North.

These and other trends create silent and unseen currents of the American economy which result in employment possibilities. American business will change, adapt, or start anew as the trends proceed and mature. Businesses and jobs will always be changing through economic expansion, and even recession, as the economy makes adjustments to move forward.

Understanding the direction the country is taking will be useful in planning the direction of your career. Pay close attention to trends in technology, industry, and politics. All future trends will have some effect on you and your career, but don't look upon these events as threats. From these movements will come opportunities, frequently with your current employer. Be watchful and be preparing to grow with your employer as the company meets the challenges of change.

In the workplace, projects will come and go, positions will open, and promotional opportunities will appear. As markets change, business will be changing the nature of its products and services. These changes will create greater needs for responsible employees. As there will always be a need for good people, there will always be places for outstanding people who are prepared!

Supply Side

You are surrounded by a vast supply of material objects, career opportunities, and caring people. The supply is limitless, but do you have a demand on this supply? Many people have many mild desires and wishes, but they do not really believe they can obtain even one of them. In fact, the supply of everything ever wished for is available to everyone.

In order to see your opportunity supply in objective terms, you must stop for a moment and think of your goals without thinking of limit or impossibilities. Ask yourself this question, "Has someone else in this world achieved the goal I have set for myself?" I would venture that the answer is, "Yes." For example, if your goal is to retire at age 60, you must acknowledge that other people have achieved this goal; if your goal is to be a happier person, you must acknowledge that other people have achieved that goal; if your goal is to earn a certain salary, you must acknowledge that someone in the business world has achieved this goal; if your goal is to complete a project, you must acknowledge that someone else could achieve that goal. There is nothing new under the sun. The supply you need to satisfy your goal is available — provided by the Law of Opportunity Supply.

Law of Opportunity Supply: EVERYTHING YOU
DESIRE IS AVAILABLE
IN UNLIMITED
QUANTITIES.

The Law of Opportunity Supply acknowledges no limitation. Every opportunity you need, want, and desire is available abundantly. You may think it impossible to obtain better job conditions or a better salary. If this is true, it isn't because there is a shortage of supply, but only because distribution of the supply doesn't favor you at this time.

As a member of the human race, you are not destined to be confined by any limitation, including poor quality of life or the struggle to earn an income. Therefore, any deficiency is in MIND only, definitely not in reality, as resources are ever-present. If you were not meant to suffer, why then do you see so much stress, so many problems, and so many failures? There has obviously been some mistake!

Demand Side

You and I possess abundant energy. We are endowed with the qualities of spirit and zest. Man is an animated being with the capacity to think, act, and achieve. Although we are full of energy, its outward expression may be limited or held back because of our thinking habits. When we remove the negative baggage, our abundant energy shines through.

Positive career growth requires personal investment of time and effort. Your contribution is centered in your thinking processes in the conscious and subconscious mind. Thoughts, emotions, and impulses are products of your childhood training and your predominant thinking patterns as an adult. The existence of these mental resources has enormous implications in your potential to place a demand on the abundant opportunity supply.

The automatic responses stored away become the energy source for growth. Looking a little closer at your mental resources, you will find that

you have energy available inside you right now,
in the form of:

THOUGHT. . . . .power to imagine, product of
                thinking, developed intention or
                plan, serious consideration
EMOTION. . . . .feeling, disturbance, excitement,
                psychic/physical reactions (anger,
                fear, love, or hate)
IMPULSE. . . . . .inspiration, motivation, force so
                communicated as to produce
                sudden motion, a sudden
                spontaneous inclination

You are energy! You are alive because you are full
of energy. Your energy becomes power when it is
harnessed and focused toward specific goals. Although you may not understand at this time why
you may respond to events with a specific emotion or impulse, you have the ability to program
your subconscious mind to convert these resources to positive demands.

To use your energy sources for successful accomplishments will take genuine effort on your
part. For the unprepared, the mental work of concentrating upon a goal for extended periods of
time can be harder than doing physical chores.
The lazy thinker finds other things to do that are
more "fun," or otherwise avoids the confrontation
with mental work. For instance, school students
can find all kinds of activities that are more ur-
gent than studying: sports, dating, television,
rock music, and sleeping. All of these things have

a place in their lives, but the serious thinkers among them will find time to hit the books, too.

Unfortunately, there are also lazy thinkers in the workplace. Many employees don't think about their goals or don't think deeply enough about their jobs. Television and sports have become an escape mechanism for employees who are unhappy with their jobs or who don't believe there is a chance of obtaining better conditions. Television and sports in themselves are not the problem; the problem is the unbalance between the employee's wish to be entertained and the employee's willingness to be challenged to think more deeply.

Mental energy is power awaiting a place to go to work. This energy can be just as intense as you want it to be. Once you know your goals, your inner power can be channeled to place a demand on the opportunity supply. Let your mental powers have a mission that is tailored to your desires. When opportunity knocks, you will recognize the knock — and you will know just what to do.

Mental Capacity

Our job conditions, whether currently negative or positive, will improve as our mental capacity expands and matures. Our present mental capacity consists of our thinking processes, memory, aptitude, and thinking skill. Employers tend

to compensate employees in proportion to their
state of professional growth and personal development, which can be correlated with the individual's mental capacity. With an increasing mental
capacity, greater job-related performances and accomplishments become possible. With these kinds
of results, employees will receive (attract) the benefits they seek. Knowing this, the key is to find a
way to increase our mental capacity.

Increasing mental capacity is a commonplace
event for children and for students pursuing an
education. The mental practice of study (concentration) and exercise is fundamental to the learning process. We recognize that the best students
are the ones who are willing to do the work and
who respect the authority of the school personnel. In a similar manner, the professional employee can achieve success in the business world
by continuing to apply these fundamentals of education.

At the heart of an individual's success lies his/
her "will" to work for success. Mental "will" is
defined as desire, wish, choice, determination, in-
sistence, and persistence. You may have read Dr.
James Dobson's book, *The Strong-Willed Child*.
Even if you haven't, the term "strong-willed"
suggests a child who is bent on doing things his/
her way. In a similar manner, employees can have
a strong will bent on improving themselves, improving job conditions, and increasing the fre-
quency of their successes. These positive events
are the result of the Law of Increase.

Law of Increase: YOUR WILL TO SUCCEED
CAUSES CONDITIONS
TO PROGRESSIVELY
IMPROVE.

Mental capacity can be increased by your will to do the work necessary for growth. Through mental exercise, the mind can be expanded. Jerry Lucas was an All-American basketball player for The Ohio State University, and played professional basketball for the New York Knicks. Mr. Lucas is now an internationally-known memory expert who has not only memorized many books, but has developed memory techniques for children. But Jerry Lucas' ability wasn't a gift; it is developed skill. As a young child, Jerry Lucas passed the time away by spelling words backwards! When traveling in the automobile on family vacations, he would mentally spell backwards the names of the objects he saw, instead of counting out-of-state license plates. Now, as an adult, he can spell the names backwards of objects he sees faster than most people can talk. Jerry Lucas' mental capacity was developed through mental exercise.

Mental exercise may come from conscious effort, as in Mr. Lucas' case, or from your job-related experiences. For example, problem-solving is an opportunity to exercise the mind as solutions are being sought. Concentrating on a problem, processing ideas, anticipating various outcomes from possible solutions, deciding on a course of action, and implementing the chosen solution is an exercise that sharpens mental skills. Building upon successes in solving little problems produces the ability to solve big problems. Our mental capacity can be increased through mental exercise if only we will exercise our "will" to do the work.

The Success Process

It has been said that the chemicals that make up our bodies are worth only 98¢. Under some circumstances, a beautiful body, or a strong body, or an agile body may have greater value. But the most important part of one's body is invaluable and irreplaceable: it is the mind. Within the mind we have the power of thinking, communicating, and living. It is this power, our mental capacity, that sets us apart from other individuals. Each person's mind is unique.

In our physical universe, equilibrium will always be the eventual condition between two tangible objects. In our "mental universe," equilibrium will always be the condition between our thoughts and the surrounding conditions. Equilibrium with conditions is a natural outcome when our developed state of mind, expressed as demand, is exposed to opportunity (the "opportunity supply"). The money, resources, and opportunities controlled by other people represent supply; our mental capacity to accomplish work and goals represents demand. In accordance with our own mental capacity, we can each make a demand on the opportunity supply. We may choose to make a casual demand on supply, or we may make a concentrated demand which increases our mental capacity and, simultaneously, increases the greatness of our accomplishments.

The rule regarding compensation for our accomplishments is that we must "be" before we "get." For example, a scientist requesting a research grant from a government agency will have more success than a high school student will; a veteran salesman already in the President's Club will have more success closing a sale than a rookie; a "best"employee will have more success getting good raises than an employee who demonstrates poor performance. These examples illustrate extreme cases where one individual is better prepared to accomplish a goal than another. The ease with which we can accomplish greater success is dependent upon our state of professional growth and personal development.

Persistence

Make a firm decision about what you want for job conditions and career goals. Set your goal and keep it in your mind until you achieve it. Being unsure of your goal or changing it constantly is futile. How can you hit a target that isn't there? If you were designing a business strategy and you changed your plan every day, you would go nowhere. Your plan would have no definite direction and would never materialize as a successful strategy.

If you plant corn seeds in your garden and you keep digging up the seeds each day to see how they are coming along, you will never harvest the crop. What you do to raise a good crop is to keep weeds out and make sure the plants get sufficient water. You have faith that the corn seeds will grow into corn plants, which will bear corn ears. Protect and nurture your thoughts and goals in the same manner. Have faith that you will reap the results you seek! If you go after your goals with intense desire, the day will come when you will see them fulfilled.

Be persistent in your thoughts and your intent. You increase the likelihood of securing your desires if you believe in them strongly enough. Oftentimes, you may want to give in. There will be times when your outlook will appear hopeless. Your job may seem endless or too great a feat to tackle, but don't give up! Have a little more patience and try just a little bit longer. Many people who have achieved a great accomplishment have felt like quitting along the way, but they didn't quit or you never would have heard of them. Thomas Edison was famous for hundreds of inventions, which he credited to his persistence. Great accomplishments are made by those who keep going until their goals are achieved.

Faith

When you truly accept that there is no lack, want, limit, or restriction of supply, you can start to receive some of its limitless, free-flowing abundance. You must have faith that what you desire can be yours, even before it has materialized in physical form or in conditions of your environment. You must build your desires within yourself. Build them in faith, with hope and courage, and hold them regardless of outside appearances. *Your success is of your own making.* If you are not satisfied with conditions as they are, you have only to visualize them as you want them in order to start the process of changing them.

Too many times, people look to the tangible environment for their basis of faith. If today's paycheck, or cash in the checking account, or other material things are accepted as the only reality, this belief shuts off the supply of greater things. Faith in the here and now becomes a security blanket. Loss of these things due to losing a job or becoming seriously ill can be traumatic for the person who doesn't understand that his/her own power to set the natural laws of human endeavor into action is his/her responsibility.

Job Security

The toughest thing we have to do is to learn to depend on our inner self for security. We have inherent mental powers that have been ignored! Most people only use ten percent of their capacity. Why haven't we used our mental powers to help ourselves? Most of us have been taught to look to someone else — to parents, to the Company, to the JOB. The job seems of paramount importance for a wage earner. *Do not let yourself lean on any thing or on any person for security.*

When your material wealth and security depend on your own state of mind, you will be healthy and happy and you will do better work. You will consider all job conditions from an "opportunity" viewpoint. For instance, if you lose a job, instead of being upset, you simply recognize an opportunity to better your conditions. When changes begin to occur, no matter what transpires, you can perceive it in one of two ways:

* You are going backwards; or
* You are going to land in a better position.

Whatever occurs will be in strict accord with your predominant state of mind. And if sometime you can't see your way clearly, do not let yourself dwell on the negative, but calmly, steadily hold a mental picture of your goal.

If you are seeking a position, keep yourself in a hopeful frame of mind and depend on your subconscious mind to guide you. Many times, what you want is hidden behind something else. Therefore, if a position that doesn't seem quite right is open for you, consider the possibility that this job may be a stepping stone to what you want. Your supply may come through the obvious channel, but natural laws of human endeavor can create any number of ways and means for you. There is no limit to the opportunity supply, but before you can benefit, you must be mentally prepared to place a demand on this supply.

Ready To Make A Demand?

Your present state of mind determines exactly what your level of professional growth and personal development is at this time. This level will not be raised just by reading this book and learning about your inherent ability to change your conditions. It isn't that simple or that fast! If you have been thinking in terms of limit or lack, you can't expect to imagine possessing a better salary, job conditions, or career opportunities *today*, and then to acquire your desire *tomorrow*.

In order to make a change in your conditions, your consciousness must change first, creating new ideas which, in turn, will make new and greater demands on your subconscious mind. Eventually, these demands will be met in accordance with the thought pattern or mental picture you hold. Just as a tree grows strong starting from a seed, you have to develop and build yourself starting from thoughts about your intense desires. You must gain skill in concentration before a new consciousness can be developed to achieve a new set of conditions.

Your progress depends on your ability to reject old ideas and set opinions. You are fortunate if you do not have many set opinions, since every association and experience you have had in the past made an impression on your subconscious. Erasing old ideas and distorted beliefs will be quicker for you, and programming new beliefs will be easier. On the other hand, if you are "set in your ways," the work required to change your consciousness will take a greater mental commitment on your part.

Learning Experience

Disappointment and times of discouragement during this process are inevitable. "Overnight success" is a myth; everything that grows takes time. In the vegetable and animal kingdoms, time is an essential ingredient for growth. For man, the change of consciousness is a learning experience that takes time. When I was a child, learning to write my own name took weeks. Learning to ride a bicycle took a few days. It took me five hours of practice to learn to land an airplane. My state of professional growth and personal development was achieved by a similar process, differing only by degree.

Every experience is beneficial if you can learn something that will increase your likelihood of success in the future. Even criticism can be a learning experience if you don't let your negative emotions interfere with the receiving of information beneficial to your well-being and future success. You can learn and grow from both trivial moments and momentous occasions. Every experience becomes a positive event if you have a definite plan that you are striving to achieve.

You may not be able to control circumstances, but you can learn to control your attitude toward circumstances. If you have a setback today, remember that tomorrow offers you another opportunity to concentrate on what you desire. Some event or circumstance may occur tomorrow that will have a personal meaning to you and will help you gain a better understanding of circumstances. Successful people use each event that creates their circumstances as a learning experience.

Fairness

Laws are no respecters of persons. Everyone has the same opportunity to be successful. If a so-called "subordinate" employee sows seeds of love and faith and a so-called "executive" employee sows seeds of fear and bigotry, you should not blame luck or others when the "subordinate" employee harvests plenty of success while the "executive" reaps bitterness and failure. There is nothing mysterious about it; law cannot discriminate. Those who work in accordance with law will get the benefits!

Remember, the supply is always equal to the demand; therefore, you must make a demand in the form of predominant thought about goals, and the supply will always be available in kind and quality of the thought seed you planted. Your character, behavior, and attitude follow the Law of Thought, Law of Mind, and Law of Cause and Effect. The conditions you find yourself in follow the Law of Recompense and the Law of Attraction. The Law of Opportunity Supply and Law of Increase combine to help you develop and grow your career into a success. By concentrating on your goals, you gain greater mental capacity that can enable you to make a greater demand on the opportunity supply.

Opportunities for achievement, recognition, career advancement, and growth will be available continually. But before you can receive, you must determine what you want and establish a demand in terms of your desire. If you want an enjoyable job, then create it in your mind first. If you want a pleasant business atmosphere, then build it with your thoughts. If you want greater financial stability, then imagine it in your mind. Nothing can be realized in physical form that is not first expressed in your thoughts. Glen Campbell made a demand on the opportunities in the entertainment field, and received for his efforts a great supply of success. In the next chapter, you will learn how to formulate demands on the limitless supply in *your* business field.

SECTION III

DO THE JOB
The "Working for Success" Plan

For many, going to work and doing the job becomes a weekly routine thought of as a necessary chore, rather than an opportunity for excitement. But doing the job with a conscious plan to achieve success can produce feelings of satisfaction, fulfillment, and excitement! The "Working for Success" Plan offers the "how-to's" you can use to achieve the career benefits you desire and more. The three keys to the Plan are *Think*, *Work*, and *Serve*.

CHAPTER 7
The First Key: Think

In the fifties, one television game show became very popular because of its large amount of prize money and the public's infatuation with the intelligence of the contestants. The show was "The $64,000 Question." The contestants would enter a sound-proof cabinet and would communicate with the show's host by means of an intercom system. Once a question was posed, the chamber would become completely silent. During the next sixty seconds, the contestant would be entirely alone to think about the question, ponder over an answer, and, finally, deliver the best answer.

We live in a pressurized, energized, and overextended world. Rarely do we take time to stop for a moment and truly think. We are "too busy cutting wood to stop and sharpen the axe"! I once asked an associate if he had time to sit down and work out some career goals. His first response was that he "thinks" about his goals, but he is so busy with work and family activities that he doesn't have time to write down his specific goals.

Have you ever heard yourself say, "I'll think about it," or, "I need more time to think about . . ."? These and other thought-provoking statements are frequently expressed by employees around the office. Many times, we make these statements because we don't know at that moment what to do, or we can't figure out the solution to a specific problem being discussed. In most cases, we know that thinking is important, but we may not understand the implications when we use the word "think." The best employees *think constructively.*

The first key to the "Working for Success" Plan is to THINK. Part of doing the job every day is basic thinking just to handle the routine tasks. Many employees stop after handling the routine, unaware of their responsibility to use their creative thinking ability to find better ways to do the job, or to create solutions to business problems. (Even if they do take this responsibility, most do not understand how to think constructively.) But employers expect to receive *mental contributions* as well as the physical presence and energetic motion of their employees.

The developed ability to think constructively will help you do the job for your employer and thereby help you to achieve your own goals. Your employer represents the most immediate source of supply to meet your income needs and to build your career success. Your performance on the job will be compensated in kind and quality of the service you provide. The THINK key shows you how to use your thinking processes to increase your mental capacity and improve the kind and quality of your service, so that you can achieve your goals and feel better about yourself.

Start with Goals

Goals represent the fulfillment of needs and desires. Your employer has business-related goals for you to achieve, such as solving a customer relations dilemma or completing a project on time. Other business-related goals may include making the best purchase of a major piece of office equipment; selection of the right candidate for an opening; or establishing the successful strategic plan for a business unit. Think about business-related goals that increase the likelihood for your employer's success.

You can establish job-related goals for yourself in this way: First, consider the Competence, Commitment, and Cooperation Components of your job performance, and their respective elements. Recognize which you must improve to insure that your job performance is the highest possible. Second, look past symptoms to see the root problem. Understand the nature of job-related problems so that you can identify permanent solutions. Third, manage your attitude so that it becomes positive and optimistic. Think about how you can improve your performance and increase your accomplishments.

Goals can also encompass "personal" issues. Improving a character trait is a worthwhile goal which will help you with relations with others at the workplace. Characteristics such as temper, impatience, anger, and stubbornness will attract negative conditions. On the other hand, when

LIFE PLAN

(1) Name _____ (2) Date _____ (3) Last Review _____

(4) My major OBJECTIVE is to: _____
_____

(5) My intermediate GOALS related to my professional growth. . . . .
    job, career, performance, problems, etc., are:

    (I will. . . . achieve, become, earn, exchange, increase,
    learn, possess. . . .)

    I will (a) _____ within 1 year.
           (b) _____ (or as desired
           (c) _____

    I will (d) _____ within 2 years.
           (e) _____ (or as desired
           (f) _____

    I will (g) _____ within 3 years.
           (h) _____ (or as desired
           (i) _____

    I will (j) _____ within 5 years.
           (k) _____ (or as desired
           (l) _____

    I will (m) _____ within 10 years.
           (n) _____ (or as desired
           (o) _____

(6) My personal GOALS related to my personal development are:

    Attitude-habits (pg. 188): (a) _____
              (b) _____
              (c) _____

    Behavior-habits (pg. 188): (d) _____
              (e) _____
              (f) _____

    Character traits (pg. 186): (g) _____
              (h) _____
              (i) _____

(7) My benefits will be (what brings me enjoyment and
    satisfaction):
              (a) _____
              (b) _____

(8) My commitment is (time each day, extra activities, etc.):
              (a) _____
              (b) _____
              (c) _____

you concentrate on positive characteristics such as passion, patience, gentleness, and helpfulness, you attract successful results. Think about the character traits that you acknowledge would make your personality one that is more positive and outgoing.

Goals are essential for your career. A career-related goal might be improving a particular job condition, such as stressful confrontations with other people, lack of recognition for a job well done, or an excessive work load. A promotion, a salary increase, a job opportunity, or success with a project may be an important goal for you. Think about the career-related goals that will lead you to be a better businessperson.

All of your goals need to be structured so that when they are achieved, you will move closer to your major objective. Remember, your major objective is the most important thing you want to accomplish during your working years. Even defining your major objective can be a goal until you finally discover the right objective for you. Think about your strengths and interests to gain some insight of what you are designed to do.

Use the Life Plan form as a guide to record your major objective, intermediate goals, and personal development goals after you finish reading this book. Write down the benefits you want to receive if you achieve your objective. How much time are you willing to commit? Remember, if you can identify a desire and define a particular goal, you have the power to see this goal fulfilled — if you pay the price. The price isn't in dollars but in the mental effort of using your thinking processes constructively, which is to process thoughts according to an organized procedure. With practice and repetitive concentration, you can direct your predominant thought to focus on your desired goals.

Concentration

Concentration need not take a great deal of effort; in fact, it can be simple and relaxing. Think, for example, of how easily you can lose yourself in a good book or a compelling television program. You become totally involved in what you are doing, and all else completely disappears from your awareness. You can train your mind to meditate in the same manner. All you have to do is consciously clear your mind of everything but the subject or situation you desire to think about.

Meditation is this deep immersion in the subject which you have chosen as your goal. When you meditate, you enter a state that opens the way for your subconscious mind to receive suggestions, ideas, and thoughts that you intentionally want to see manifested. This mental exercise gives you control over your state of mind, and a means to change as you mentally prepare for greater success.

You can start right now by turning your attention to how you can do your job better; how you can do it more efficiently; how you can improve your product, service, ideas, or relationships; how you can improve your skills, talents, and abilities. Your power of thought is a creative resource that can dramatically help you in your daily efforts to be successful.

If you lift weights every day, your muscles get stronger. Clinical tests have conclusively demonstrated that mental exercise causes the brain to grow in capability. Remember, the laws of human endeavor can be set into motion by your mental powers. The basic steps to increase your mental capacity are outlined below:

First, you make up your mind that you can condition yourself into any attitude, response, or habit you desire;

Second, you create for yourself the goals you want to achieve, and the attitude-habits, behavior-habits, and character traits that will achieve them;

Third, you train your subconscious mind by daily practice.

These simple steps can exercise the mind and increase its capacity for the disciplined employee. An undisciplined thinker will permit a bombardment of things seen, heard, and sensed to make impressions on the subconscious mind. These impressions may hinder one's mental development.

On the other hand, the disciplined thinker will use concentration to imagine goals accomplished, and decide which observable stimuli are permitted to impress his/her subconscious mind. Daily practice of concentration produces impressions that lead to successful experiences.

Concentration is the tool that can change the world you have into the world you want. Concentration brings the subconscious mind and the conscious mind together for the purpose of accomplishing a goal. Whether the goal is to improve job performance, solve a problem, improve an attitude or behavior, or build character, concentration is a mental resource that can accelerate the creative process.

Each day, spend a short period of time, even a couple of minutes, in the process of meditation. This time is called QUIET, because the best time to meditate and concentrate is a private time when distractions can be avoided. This technique offers a practical means for you to use your mental powers to accomplish more and achieve more success.

The QUIET Technique

QUIET is a silent, relaxing time when you can turn thoughts inward. Nothing unusual or out of the ordinary will occur during QUIET. It is a time of creativity and building, which you control. You will be alone with the real you, unaided by any crutch or superficial priorities. Now is the time to do *hard mental work*!

Control of the mind is attainable first through control of the body. For a set period of time each day, go to a room that you have chosen for complete relaxation. Lie on a comfortable sofa or sit in your favorite chair. Relax your entire body by becoming very still, closing your eyes, and thinking a while about each part of your body becoming very relaxed — almost as if you were going to sleep. Then think about enjoyable memories, beautiful places you have seen, and pleasant times to come. Allow all pressures to leave your body and know that you have plenty of time to think about your goals.

Complete relaxation will not be easy at first, but with continued practice, it will become very natural. In fact, you will look forward to your time alone for directing your body to relax and allowing your frustrations to evaporate. Eventually, you will be able to direct your body to relax in any surroundings and under any conditions. When you have mastered this technique, you will gain tremendous confidence and extreme bodily poise.

Controlling your thoughts can be as easy as controlling your body. At first, it will seem difficult to keep your mind on one subject for an extended period of time, but eventually it will become effortless. Your thoughts are used to

THE QUIET TECHNIQUE
"How to Think Constructively"

Control Your Body

1. Retire to a place where you will not be disturbed.
2. Seat yourself comfortably.
3. Relax every muscle.
4. Close your eyes.
5. Be still.

Control Your Thoughts

6. Think about pleasant things for a moment.
7. Concentrate on your goal.
8. Listen to your thoughts.
9. Continue to concentrate.

Control Your Actions

10. Open your eyes.
11. Move about.
12. Act upon your ideas and thoughts.
13. Believe that you have achieved your goal.
14. Continue the process daily.

jumping from one subject to the next. Select a subject (goal) that you wish to think about and hold it in your mind for a few minutes. If your thoughts stray, call them back to your subject as soon as you perceive the change. (You will be aware of your surroundings in a detached sort of way.)

Set a time goal for your concentration. Even ten minutes will be a great accomplishment. This effort may be easier for some than for others, but in time you will be able to control your thoughts for as long as you desire. You have a task of concentration, and you are accomplishing it. You are controlling your body and your mind.

With your eyes closed and your mind concentrating on your chosen subject (major objective, specific goal, problem, attitude-habit or behavior-habit, or character trait), see the object of your desire from many different perspectives. If you desire a specific job assignment, see yourself doing the job. Imagine the job situation as you would like it and, repeatedly, ask questions of yourself on how you can get this job. Or, if you need to solve a problem, think of the problem in respect to the facts you know, and, repeatedly, ask questions of yourself about the root source of the problem (or a possible solution if you know the root problem).

After some period of concentration, just remain still. In this silent time, just listen to your thoughts as they come and go. Answers or ideas frequently come to you either at this moment or later when you may least expect it. As you "hear" ideas on how you may accomplish your goal, pick up on these thoughts and shift your concentration time to focus on the new direction indicated. Through this development process, you will find the path you should take to accomplish your goal.

You will know when it is enough for that session. At that time, you will open your eyes, sit up, feel refreshed, and go about your business with more energy and determination. This experience can become a power-building time that is enjoyable and satisfying. You have discovered how to develop the motivational engine that will drive you through good and bad times as you work for success.

Power Time

The most effective time to concentrate on your goals is prior to sleep or just after you wake up in the morning. The reason for this is that the subconscious is extremely accessible when you are in a "sleepy" mood. The subconscious is busy continuously even when you are asleep. You can easily prove your subconscious power by trying the time-keeping experiment.

First, think about the occasions when you were extremely concerned that you would not awaken in time to make an important business appointment. You may have set your alarm clock for 7:00 a.m., but you mysteriously awakened at 6:59 a.m. just before your alarm went off! You may not have realized it, but this was your subconscious functioning for a practical purpose. You had subconsciously instructed your mind that you wished to awaken at a certain time, and you did.

Next, test this power for yourself *consciously*. Tell yourself the exact time you wish to arise in the morning, and concentrate on it for a few minutes. Repeat this self-talk instruction just before you fall asleep, and you will awaken on time. If this does not work for you the first time you try it, try again. Your mental abilities are so precise that you do not need a clock. The "alarm clock" example demonstrates how your thinking can affect your conditions. You thought — you achieved!

One Source Of Wisdom

You have undoubtedly experienced delayed memory recall. You may have remembered a person's name or some other detail some time after you tried your hardest to recall it. This is a perfect example of your subconscious supplying you with information that you requested. The experience of your entire life is available to you once you develop the mental capacity to control your thought processes. The memory bank centered in your subconscious has stored information that you have read, heard, and seen throughout your life.

Thinking constructively uses the knowledge and information stored away in the subconscious mind to bring action ideas out to your conscious mind. When working on a difficult project or a complex problem for any length of time, I find thinking constructively prior to sleep frequently results in waking up in the night or the next morning with an idea or a possible answer that will lead me to a successful outcome. If I focus on my career goals, I may receive an idea to act upon the next day that will move me closer to my major objective.

When you think constructively — when you concentrate with a definite purpose and technique — you evoke the force needed to break into your reservoir of knowledge, experience, and understanding. For you, this is an immediate source of wisdom to assist in making decisions. Some decisions may require you to seek out more information than you have been exposed to in the past, but your accumulated wisdom will lead you to get any help you need.

Better Job Performance

You can use QUIET to improve your performance on the job. Begin by establishing your goal, using the evaluation technique presented in

Chapter 1. You have to become aware of your strengths and weaknesses first before you can hope to make significant changes. One of your goals may be to increase your sensitivity to daily successes and failures relating to your work or your relationships with other people. Concentrate on the elements that make up the Components of Performance: Competence, Commitment, and Co-operation.

Set realistic and meaningful goals that, when achieved, will most increase your overall performance. You may think of specific goals suggested by the Job Performance Guideline chart on page 180. For example, you may have a personality conflict with an associate, and you may believe the fault lies with the other person. Previously, your pride and feeling that you are right have prevented a solution to this stressful and frustrating dilemma. But, by concentrating on the admiration element of the Cooperation Component, you begin the process of improving the relationship and removing the burden of responsibility for the conflict from yourself.

If your behavior of respectfulness and submissiveness does not produce positive results in a reasonable time, then the other person's thinking process is responsible — not yours! The Law of Recompense and the Law of Attraction will compensate the other person with the exact conditions they are subconsciously asking for. When you are mentally prepared, the stubborn, uncooperative,

JOB PERFORMANCE

Guideline

Competence Component

* More product or job *knowledge:* course, training class, conferring with experienced associates.
* Better *skills* with hands or mental processes: supervising people, making decisions, solving problems, typing and word processing skills.

Commitment Component

* Greater *confidence* in your abilities and talents; belief in your own self-worth.
* Greater *motivation* to try harder to achieve worthwhile goals and prove your value to your employer.

Cooperation Component

* Greater *helpfulness to* other associates; volunteer to assist, encourage, greet, and share work before being asked.
* More *admiration* toward associates; radiate feelings of sincere caring and good will.

obstinate, and belligerent personalities can't hurt you or your performance.

Remember, negative conditions are the results of thought. Your negative thought can be changed by erasing old ideas and distorted beliefs, and programming new positive thought by using QUIET. You cannot control others' thinking processes, but you can control what you think, and the state of mind you want to have. QUIET is your *personal success secret*, which you can use to be a more sensitive person — one who looks objectively at conditions. You will soon know which elements you must concentrate on to improve your job performance and relations with others.

Problem-Solving Skill

Too few employees realize that problems provide an opportunity to contribute both to their company's and to their own growth. Many will complain and curse the problems of the business or of their jobs, but very few will take the initiative to work out solutions for the problems that plague the day-to-day operations.

When you realize (1) that problems are a way of life, and (2) that you have the inherent power to solve them, your perspective about facing problems will change. You will see problems as imperfections created by imperfect thought or lack of thought. Problems can be solved by using the

PROBLEM-SOLVING GUIDE

Root Problem	Possible Problem Areas	Possible Solutions
LEADERSHIP		
	Awareness	Listen, observe, encourage
	Desire	Focus, commit, persist
	Initiative	Be first, self-starter
	Decisiveness	Investigate, think, decide
	Courage	Face problems, do the right thing
	Objectivity	Set high standards, use facts
MOTIVATION		
	Interest	Match employees with job assignments that intrigue and challenge
	Enthusiasm	Provide immediate feedback on employee's performance; conduct timely "formal" reviews
COMMUNICATIONS		
	Understanding	Explain company and project goals, ideas, directions
	Media	Use clear and concise written and oral instructions; conduct short meetings that keep on track
CHANGE	Fear	Greater employee involvement, communications, planning, participation
PRODUCTIVITY		
	Waste	Use accurate documentation
	Bottlenecks	Attention to employee placement, training, tools
	Diversions	Establish procedures, policies

power of thought. With mental exercise, your problem-solving skill can be improved. In addition, your confidence and self-worth will increase as a natural product of solving business- and job-related problems successfully.

To solve business concerns and job dilemmas permanently, think in terms of the five root problems: Leadership, Motivation, Communications, Change, and Productivity. Remember, the results of these problems are only symptoms when you look objectively at the observable and measurable negative conditions that need to be fixed. From the simple to the most complex, undesirable conditions surrounding your job or your employer's business can be traced to one or more elements of the five basic problems. The Problem-Solving Guide may help you to identify some possible solutions.

Solving problems becomes a natural process if you routinely follow an organized method when faced with business concerns or job-related dilemmas. To solve your root problems, practice this simple procedure:

First, define the problem to be solved in specific terms. Start with the symptoms you observe; then, look for the root problem.

Second, gather all the facts regarding the problem. Consciously think about these facts, and ponder whether other questions must be answered before a conclusion should be reached.

Third, list all the possible solutions that occur to your conscious mind. By association, more ideas may be evoked that may lead you to the right solution.

Fourth, if the right solution or set of actions isn't obvious at this point, *take the problem into QUIET.* Let your subconscious mind give you the solution.

In QUIET, visualize the problem, and concentrate on the goal of finding a solution. If you find that an answer does not materialize while you are in QUIET, release the problem to your subconscious mind and let it simmer for a few days. Your subconscious mind will keep working on the problem while you go about your business. Then, when you might least expect it, an answer will come into your awareness. The seed was planted in the subconscious while concentrating in QUIET, but the crop will be harvested in your conscious awareness.

In time you can freely go into and come out of QUIET as you need to write down ideas, and even concentrate with your eyes open as you may need to in meetings and discussions with associates. (Don't overlook using brainstorming sessions with others to test your solution or to gather more information helpful to your cause.) By using this simple problem-solving procedure, you will exercise your thinking skill, which is necessary to solve the most complex problems that you face at work.

The Perfect Attitude

It is your mental attitude that gives you control over your job, career, and feelings of happiness. You can exercise positive control for success, or you can allow negative conditions to exist just by being mentally lazy. When you realize that the mental realm is the realm of true reality, you view events, circumstances, and conditions in an entirely new light. Your effort to use QUIET to concentrate upon Character Qualities of Performance (see page 186) becomes one of the most important activities in your business life.

QUIET is a place where you can develop a belief in the possibility that you can achieve your goals. Concentrate on the qualities of hope, faith, integrity, honesty, optimism, courage, initiative, generosity, tolerance, tact, and kindness. Know that the natural laws of human endeavor are working for you 24 hours a day. QUIET is a means for you to use predominant thought to make suggestions (specific demands) to your subconscious mind to serve as a pattern to work for — to place a demand on the supply. Set a goal of developing a perfect attitude for success as a top priority. Strive every day to transform learned positive attitude traits into mental skills.

Your job conditions, career success, and personal happiness can be improved by using QUIET as a constructive time for evaluation and building. Before you blame luck or other people for your

CHARACTER QUALITIES OF PERFORMANCE

Positive Attitude

Competence Component

Common Sense	Open-mindedness	Realism
Discipline	Optimism	Teachability
Flexibility	Organization	Understanding
Inventiveness	Originality	Vision

Commitment Component

Competitiveness	Dependability	Initiative
Courage	Determination	Passion
Credibility	Eagerness	Promptness
Dedication	Enthusiasm	Tenacity

Cooperation Component

Attentiveness	Honesty	Obedience
Caring	Humbleness	Patience
Courtesy	Integrity	Sincerity
Friendliness	Kindness	Trustworthine

negative conditions, make every effort to get your own house in order. You have not done your best unless you reach deep inside of yourself and use your mental powers to the maximum. QUIET provides the means for you to get your attitude right, thereby separating your self-worth from the external events, conditions, and circumstances that you cannot control directly.

Barriers

Fear can be your worst enemy. It can destroy your progress very easily just when you start to grow stronger. Have confidence in your ability to increase your mental capacity. Replace destructive thoughts with constructive thoughts, and let new positive feelings overpower negative emotions and impulses. *Practice success habits daily* (see page 188).

If you start to have doubts or if problems come up, create a positive affirmation to handle any negative tendency or fear. The affirmation or suggestion is a statement of what you want to happen. A helpful affirmation to repeat to yourself is, "I will achieve my goal. I have the power. Nothing can keep me from it." Remember, the subconscious mind accepts all information as true; it does not reject or even consider the material it is given. Your subconscious mind simply acts upon the thoughts and desires with which it is presented.

SUCCESS HABITS

Examples

Attitude-habits:

- Think only positive thoughts
- Be more optimistic
- Be careful of what you see and hear
- Speak only positive thoughts
- Wish only success for others
- Practice only positive attitude traits
- Use "self-help" affirmations

Behavior-habits:

- Walk a little faster
- Smile more
- Be interested in things about you
- Practice QUIET technique daily
- Listen to others
- Praise others
- Address people by name

The subconscious mind is part of your nervous system. It can't reason or judge, but can only accept conscious thought impressions as true. So as you go through the transformation process to change your thinking, don't be afraid to do some acting. Go about your business acting as if you have already received the new conditions that would be yours if you achieved your goals. This kind of conscious behavior will impress your subconscious mind just as directly as your affirmations. So, smile more, walk a little faster, and show some elements of the life you want your subconscious mind to work for.

Think Constructively

Your creative thoughts represent a significant contribution in the workplace. Not only will you do a better job if you think constructively about business- and job-related problems, but you can also be the source of inspiration for other associates as they witness your attitude and behavior through your actions and demeanor.

Set yourself apart from the many people who go to work each day, put in their time on the job, and then rush out to "play" as soon as possible. You can take quality time each day to THINK about job needs, problems that need solutions, associates who need your help, customers who need your support, and the needs of your employer to achieve company goals. Time spent in the doctor's waiting room, at the railroad crossing waiting on a train, and waiting in line at the checkout counter can become productive and creative opportunities. Take a 15-minute-per-day break to think in QUIET, or take any time your mind can turn inward to concentrate on your job performance, business problems, and the needs of others.

Not only can you do the job by thinking constructively, you can achieve your personal goals by using the same process. The natural laws of human endeavor will be set into motion when you use QUIET to concentrate on these goals. You have the power to accomplish the goals that are important to your employer, to your job, and to your career growth. So, *DO* the job by THINKING constructively.

CHAPTER 8
The Second Key: Work

Visualize this situation: Your boss comes up to you at noon and asks you to complete a particular rush assignment by 8:00 a.m. the next day. This assignment normally takes two days. After the boss walks away, what is your first thought? Would you say to yourself things such as "What exactly must I do to get this assignment done on time?" or "Who could help me to cut the time?" If this circumstance happened to you, would you ignore the request, or would you put your mind to it and find a way to get the job done as well as possible?

"Putting your mind to it" is an essential part of doing the work your employer expects. But equally important, you are more likely to have an enjoyable work experience if you use both your physical and mental resources to their fullest. In this manner, your work represents an important part of your life not because you have to work, but because you are mentally involved with the work process. When you put your mind to anything you deem important, you are involved and committed. The best employees *work diligently*.

The second key to the "Working for Success" Plan is to WORK. The top executives in any field become fully involved in what they are doing. They choose their careers and achieve their desired success partly because they sincerely ENJOY what they're doing. In short, they have a tremendous, positive attitude, which changes a job from one of monotonous drudgery to joy. When comedian George Burns was asked why he worked so hard and so long for so many years, he said he loved his partner (wife Gracie Allen), he loved the theatre, and he loved the audience. Mr. Burns enjoys what he is doing and, although in his nineties, he is *still* going strong!

The Law of Attraction says that if you enjoy every relationship and situation, you will attract others to your aid. If you are personally interested in the type of work you do, you will radiate feelings of commitment and confidence which will, in turn, attract conditions that you enjoy. So, find work that you are interested in, put your every effort into doing it well, and share your joy with others.

Enjoyable Work

Use QUIET to help discover the right kind of work for you — work that will be enjoyable, rewarding, and fulfilling. The answer to "What *is* that work?" lies within you right now. You can discover your role in the business world if you set a goal to learn what it is that would give you purpose and direction. There are three steps to find out what would be an enjoyable career for you.

The first step is to find out what type of work

you really enjoy. It is possible to find yourself in a rut and assume you are enjoying what you are doing. But an honest look at your feelings may help you to discover the difference. For instance, engineering appealed to me because I enjoyed solving technical problems and creating designs that worked.

The second step in achieving an enjoyable career is to specialize in some particular branch of work. Learn as much as you possibly can regarding your field of interest. Be enthusiastic as you learn all that is available. If possible, you should know more than anyone else in some particular facet of the business. Become your company's expert. I found that instrumentation and electronics engineering work associated with process control systems were of more interest to me than electrical power design or any other branch of engineering (such as chemical, aeronautical, or mechanical).

The last step is the most important one: You must be sure that what you choose to do does not serve your success only. Your desire must not be entirely selfish; it must benefit humanity. The flow of good from you must go forth with the ultimate purpose of helping others. In turn, good will be returned to you by some channel. With the right kind of motive, this thinking can lead to enjoyable and rewarding experiences. My engineering career led to a business management career wherein I was able to help more customers. Through my efforts and those of my associates, my customers' productivity problems were being solved. My customers were able to stay competitive with better quality products and lower costs of production, and to continue providing jobs to their employees.

When considering an enjoyable career for yourself, ask yourself two key questions:

1. Will the rewards be based on performance?
2. Will the job expand as my abilities increase?

If the answer to both these questions is yes, then the career you are considering could lead you along the path of growth. Talk with others who can help you. Learn all that you can about the job you desire. Then use QUIET to discover how you can use your talents and abilities to be worthy of appointment to the job of your dreams.

With persistence, faith, and time, a feeling for your "right kind of work" will come to you. After a period of testing and questioning, this feeling will eventually become more defined and focused. For some, this process of setting a goal of finding the right job, career, and place in the business world may come quickly; for others, it may take months. But, once you *do* know what you want to do, start to work mentally to do it!

Personal Pride

Be proud of yourself! You are a unique person, with a combination of talents and abilities that only you possess. You have worth to yourself and others. The negative conditions surrounding many employees at work, or in personal matters, create for each the wrong self-image. Most do not understand the incredible truth that *each human being is a wonderfully created spirit.* Look closer — you have abilities, talents, skills, dreams, emotions, and more. You have the ability to think and visualize, and you have a moral conscience.

When you think about the fact that you and I were nothing before our parents conceived us, how great it is that you and I now each have mental power, a physical body, and life-moving energy. Our tongues and lips have the flexibility to form words, and our brains understand them, but this ability is denied to all other animals. No other creature on this earth can do what we can when we fully use all our resources.

Being proud is to have feelings of self-worth, self-respect, and self-confidence. At the office, pride becomes personal dignity and inner satisfaction in a job well done. This satisfaction doesn't require the roar of the crowd or frequent strokes from your supervisor. With the right kind of mental preparation, you can become personally secure, which releases you from the tangible conditions surrounding you (e.g., criticisms, negative job conditions, and failures).

Believe In Success

Go to sleep feeling successful every night; use QUIET to reinforce the idea of success every day;

be consistent in your effort; and you will eventually implant the idea of success in your subconscious mind. Believe that you were born to succeed. *You were never meant to be a failure or suffer negative conditions.* (The natural laws of human endeavor are no respecters of persons, and abundance is the natural law of the universe.) To help you embrace a hopeful state of mind, repeat this affirmation to yourself frequently, and especially whenever doubt creeps in: "This job will lead me to the success I desire."

If you are seeking a promotion in your work, imagine your supervisor, associates, and customers congratulating you on your promotion. Make the picture vivid and clear. Hear the voices, see the gestures, and feel the reality of it all. Think and act in the same manner you will when you get the appointment. Continue to do this frequently, with continual concentration, and you will likely experience the joy of being promoted to the desired position (or by some channel, attract an equivalent position).

On the other hand, if you are silently worrying, resentful, and unhappy about being underpaid and under-appreciated, then you are subconsciously severing your ties with the organization. You are setting in motion the Law of Cause and Effect, and this law will create a negative result. Your supervisor may eventually say to you, "We have to let you go." Actually, you let *yourself* go! The supervisor was simply the instrument through which your own negative mental state was confirmed. The circumstance of being fired had its beginning in your mind. The "cause" was your negative thought and the "effect" was the response of your supervisor — the negative result guaranteed by the Law.

Positive progress in your job development and career growth can be assured only by positive thought. Allow no negative thoughts to reside in your mind. If you have honest feelings of despair about your job or your performance, then it is your responsibility to discuss the subject with your supervisor. Only by open discussion with your supervisor can you set in motion the Law of Recompense. You have the ability to plant thought seeds in your supervisor's mind! Plant quality seeds about your goals. In most situations, the supervisor will accept positive input, and over time, your positive input will accelerate the materialization of positive changes in your job conditions.

Importance Of Pay

Many people think that it would be unwise to leave a job where they receive adequate pay. They dislike the possibility of taking a pay cut. Remember, pay is a short-term compensation. People who earn the higher salaries are those who ENJOY their positions and seek employment that is challenging and fulfilling. Do not place your faith in your starting pay, but in your potential income!

Always think ahead, and concentrate on your potential. Think of what you can be, not what you are today. Try not to concern yourself with immediate rewards. Career satisfaction and financial rewards will come naturally if you are doing work you truly enjoy and you are providing superior services to others. Your contribution as an employee will be rewarded, whether by an obvious or by an unexpected channel, as the result of working in accord with law. Prepare yourself mentally, and you won't be afraid to make a commitment to your future.

Earning Raises

Being a conscientious employee will pay off. Arrive at the office on time each day, be dependable, be loyal, and strive to be one of the best employees. Keep your mind focused on the job and the duties you are paid to perform. Resist the temptation to dwell on your financial situation or to criticize company policies and pay practices. These things are important to your well-being, but do not let these concerns interfere with your productive efforts to perform the job to the best of your ability.

It is not uncommon for some people to let their personal spending habits or life styles get them into trouble. I have heard it said by these people that there is "more month than there is paycheck." Many times, the pressures to meet one's financial commitments motivate the individual to express demands upon the employer to pay more salary for the job. These employees tend to relate the amount of the raise more to their needs rather than to their actual performance and accomplishments.

You must understand that your supervisor *wants* to give you a raise. Your boss will not gain in the long run by underpaying employees. To receive more, your performance and accomplishments must be worth more. Increase your abilities to accomplish more, be enthusiastic, and extend yourself to help others. Not only will raises be attracted to you, you will also be guaranteed a job in times of recession and promoted in times of economic growth.

Your raise may come by some expected channel; that is, your current supervisor. But it may also come from some other unexpected channel: improved fringe benefits, stock award, a new employer. The salary compensation increase is inevitable if that is what you desire and you produce great service that merits the reward. You must first be certain that you have mentally raised your consciousness to a level that truly makes you a better performer, a more capable thinker, and a successful achiever; in other words, a valuable employee.

Need For Employees

The classified section of your local newspaper is adequate proof that service is always needed. Just take a look at the want ads! Advertising sections have endless lists of available positions that change every single day. Almost any occupation you can think of has an opening. The most evident needs are for service employees in the local retail and restaurant businesses, but these and other corporations also need good clerical, technical, administrative, and managerial help.

There will never be a shortage of jobs. If you want to work, there is a place for you in the vast business world. The Law of Opportunity Supply guarantees that there is work for you somewhere, either within your current employer's organization or elsewhere. In fact, the demand for the "best" employees is greater than the supply.

However, in spite of the enormous number of jobs available, there are still millions of people out of work each and every day. Too many people see the jobs that are available as pointless or without a future. Or they think that competition is too tough. Or they are not willing to adjust their standard of living to match their present earning power.

Jobs *are* available that are compatible with your state of professional growth and personal development. There are employment needs that are not advertised or handled by employment recruiting firms. If you are seeking a new job and wish to find these potential opportunities, observe the types of businesses that are advertising for entry-level jobs. It is possible to conclude that one of these companies (or another department with your current employer) will need the particular types of skills and abilities you possess. Remember, in the areas of management and professional positions, the exact job may not even be defined or justified *until the right person comes along*! So look past that advertising listing or that starting job to the career opportunity you seek. Plant thought seeds of what you want, let as many people as you can know what you are interested in, and, eventually, the right job for you will become available.

Whether you are between jobs or working your way through jobs to get to where you want to be, substitute the hope of accomplishing your goal for worry and stress. Use QUIET to prepare yourself so that you can recognize that "interim" job that is right for you now, and will in time lead you to the job you prefer. Continue to use QUIET and work at your present job until you find your place in the business world and fulfill your *chosen* destiny.

Job Stress

While you are preparing yourself for greater success, take some time to further eliminate stress as you perform your present assignment. You or others you know may complain about job stress or job burn-out. Stress is a reality, and millions of America's workers are spending billions of our country's dollars on cures. Doctors recommend endless lists of treatments for possible relief. Many people walk, jog, or run. Many take muscle relaxants as regularly as they change their diets. The cure is right in front of them, yet it often goes unnoticed: the solution to your job stress is *you*!

You will likely spend more of your waking hours in your office than you will at home. You will probably spend more time at your desk chair than in your comfortable rocking chair, so spend this valuable time doing what you enjoy. If you don't like your job, then it will reflect in the quality of your life. You will not like yourself if you don't like anything about what you spend the majority of your time doing.

When you are doing the right kind of work, you will be amazed at how you handle stressful events and circumstances. You are committed, involved, and you have your sights set on higher goals for yourself. Stress is a mistake that is caused by thought (possibly by others' thinking). But, since you know now that stress is the result of thought, you also know that this condition can be erased by thought — *your* thinking!

When you think you are overloaded and overlooked, you will attract even more conditions similar to your negative perception. Instead, you can use constructive thinking as a habit to change your mental attitude about ringing phones, excessive workloads, criticism from others, and lack of attention from management. Those situations can be irritations, or they can be opportunities for you to prove your developed abilities. A deep commitment to your goals and to the good of others will bring about a hopeful mental attitude that will not permit stressful circumstances to occupy any space or time in your mind.

Starting A New Assignment

Seeking a new assignment or job is an important first effort toward improving your conditions, but you must continue those efforts once you get the appointment. Getting off to a good start is extremely important. First impressions last a long time, and early relationships, good and bad, color your work enjoyment for years to come. Knowing a few basic principles can avert emotional trauma and speed success.

CONCENTRATE. Plan to give your job 110 percent of your time and energy for the first month or two. Enlist your family's support so that they will understand that your job will become your top priority for a while.

KNOW WHAT IS EXPECTED. What is your job? Precisely what are you expected to know and to do? Find out! If you are unsure of your responsibilities, ask questions. Assume nothing, and take notes along the way. Ignorance is tolerated when you are new, but it is inexcusable later.

LEARN HOW TO DO THE JOB. Every job has its peculiarities. Ask questions or directions. It is better to ask than to make a costly mistake. Accept advice from senior associates. Be a good listener instead of trying to show others you know it all.

DEVELOP RELATIONSHIPS. Get acquainted with your associates; they are generally more approachable when you are new. You can ask them questions and seek help. Don't waste company time talking about personal matters, but take every opportunity to communicate about relevant business. This will lay the foundation for enjoyable working conditions and for a future opportunity to return their help.

"GO THE EXTRA MILE." Don't be afraid to put in extra hours and extra effort. Aim for a quality performance. You will not be able to make increased efforts all the time, but it is possible to go all out for the first few weeks or months on your job. Early total effort will provide good job "insurance."

BE A FINISHER. Unfinished work helps no one. You cannot sell a half-made product. Therefore, develop a reputation for finishing what you start, and finish it on time! By earning a reputation for dependability, you will model the character of a valuable employee.

Applying these simple principles will set the standard for your continued performance. The Law of Attraction will be at work, for your employer will view you as a hard-working team player. Companies are always in need of such performers and will, in most situations, try harder to provide the kind of environment they (you!) like.

Workaholics

Burning the midnight oil can lead to accomplishments, but it can also lead to becoming a compulsive workaholic. Hard work is necessary when you have a task to complete, but there are definite dangers involved in working too hard for too long. First, many employees tend to get numb after spending a good amount of time on a task. Failure to take a break and "recharge the batteries" will hamper enthusiasm and creativity. Second, if employees acquire the long-hours habit, there is always tonight or this weekend (free time usually needed for family and personal relaxation) to tackle writing that report, estimating that quote, or answering those letters. Finally, there is the exorbitant price that many of us pay for this type of behavior. Breakdowns, illness, divorce, alcoholism, and premature death are all too common among those who buy the "midnight oil" programs.

So, work hard! The more you put in, the more you'll get back! But remember: there's a fine line between working diligently and working obsessively. By giving your career your whole-hearted attention, you will have a strong sense of accomplishment and pride in your ability, but always keep your career endeavors in balance with the other elements of your life. Take periodic breaks, schedule vacations, leave your weekends open, read books that interest you, and take quality time with the family.

Positive Frame Of Mind

Increase your self-worth by directing your energies in one direction and letting all unproductive diversions (thoughts, emotions, circumstances, events, etc.) fall away. Negative relationships, bad tempers, unconstructive thoughts, and destructive emotions cause great unhappiness and poor health. Discouragement and failure were not meant to be a part of your life. Through positive relationships and small successes, you will find the success you seek.

Keep your own counsel! Informing your fellow associates of your personal goals will not increase your success; it only wastes your valuable time and permits people to criticize your ideas too soon. (One-on-one discussions with your supervisor regarding your performance and career goals are encouraged as a means to communicate your interest and to plant seeds of what you want.) You will accomplish your task if you keep important personal plans to yourself. Think about associates who continuously chatter about what they are going to do. How often do they actually *do* anything? Private thoughts will stimulate your creativity and motivational forces by making impressions onto your subconscious mind. The more you talk to yourself, the more you will achieve.

Procrastination

Procrastination is putting off intentionally and habitually the doing of something that should be done. It is a negative trait which exists in all of us to some degree. I have worked hard to eliminate this trait in myself, and still I have the urge every once in awhile to "put off until tomorrow" instead of making a little more effort to take action; instead of placing that call, meeting with that customer, or thinking about that problem just a little more.

I used to rationalize this lack of action with various excuses: don't have time, don't know how to do it, it's not my job, etc. Unfortunately for me, I was disguising the real source of my procrastination by making excuses. The real source of my procrastination was that the things I put off or delayed just simply weren't my priorities. This kind of thinking was the result of my not understanding the importance of the task to my employer and to my personal growth. Now, with this understanding, I have learned to set daily goals and strive to complete them. This method has helped me to be a self-starter and get things done quickly.

However, "procrastination" in one sense can be an effective tool in solving complicated problems, or in resolving issues that have a significant impact on people or business strategies. Finding facts, listening to the ideas of others, testing some possible solutions may lead to a better understanding of the problem. Using QUIET to concentrate upon the goal of finding a solution or course of action, then letting it simmer, may be termed "procrastination," but the results will likely be better than if a hasty decision was executed.

Dependability

There is a necessary relationship among all people who work in the business world. The stockholders depend upon the company management, the company management depends upon the employees, the employees depend upon each other, and the customers depend upon *all* of them! As an employee, you depend upon associates throughout your company, and upon the employees of your suppliers. Everywhere you turn, people give and take each other's time, ideas, and services.

A major element of dependability is the fulfillment of personal commitments to complete a specific task or assignment. Once you understand how a missed commitment by you affects others' ability to do their jobs, you must dig in mentally to motivate and drive yourself to make your commitments. With a reputation of consciously working hard to complete your commitments, you build a successful track record that attracts success to you.

Self-Motivation

The internal drive to work diligently is a mental trait that comes from the right kind of thinking. It comes when the mind is developed to the degree that it becomes a natural behavior to work steadily, earnestly, and energetically. At work, plant seeds of "can do" and "possibility" thinking in your subconscious mind when doing your job. Plant thought seeds of support, encouragement, and cooperation toward your associates. Always see your job and career as positive and fulfilling.

When I was living on the family farm, I was expected to do chores each day and work a full day every Saturday all year. My view of all this physical labor was negative, to say the least. Farming was very hard work, and it didn't appear to me at the time that this work would lead to anything worthwhile. Instead of staying after school to participate in sports or working for other farmers for pay, it was my destiny to work at home for "free."

My minimal level of motivation was obvious as

I would reluctantly do the farm chores Dad told me to do, but when Saturday night came around, you would see a new me! I would rush to take a shower, dress, grab Dad's car keys, and be gone. Now I was self-motivated because I was doing what I wanted to do — and it was fun!

Work can be fun, and it will be if you do the mental work to discover what it is you love to do, and then do it. My dad loved farming, and he didn't look for other means of making a living when prices were down or the crops didn't yield well. He stuck it out, finding different and more modern ways to produce products for sale.

Additionally, he really enjoyed riding a tractor for long hours throughout all kinds of weather. Dad used these hours to mentally plan and visualize what he had to do in the next day, next week, and next years to be a successful farmer. Dad was a successful businessman who used his mental talents and physical abilities to the fullest doing what he loved to do. Dad was self-motivated by his interest in his work, and by the satisfaction of being one of best farmers in America.

Work Diligently

As an employee, you should want to work in an organization that has leaders with intense desire to make the business successful; leaders who strive for excellence in products and services; leaders who are competitive in getting orders and seeking business opportunities. These leaders provide an environment for learning and growth that will help you to be a better and more successful businessperson.

Give your employer, at the very minimum, a day's work for a day's pay. By learning to think constructively, and by working diligently, you will come to be among the most valuable employees. Work hard, do the extras, be confident in your abilities, and look forward to your successful future. *DO* the job by WORKING diligently!

CHAPTER 9
The Third Key: Serve

Men and women in military service have the highest ideal of the "serve" concept: they serve their country with their lives. In combat, a soldier sets aside his feelings of fear and, if necessary, sacrifices his life to accomplish the mission. This supreme commitment serves the benefits of fellow soldiers and the citizens back home. Due to this kind of service, wars are won and freedom is maintained.

The supreme sacrifices necessary to win wars differ from those needed to be successful in business. But serving associates, superiors, and customers has a similar characteristic: providing a service for the benefit of another even when one has to give up something very important. Typically, in business one gives time, knowledge, support, and, possibly, money. The best employees *serve unselfishly.*

The third key to the "Working for Success" Plan is to SERVE. Serving others is an action that works under control of the Compensation Laws. You have a limitless supply of caring and compassion when you have the right mental attitude. By replacing self-centered thoughts with thoughts directed to others, you radiate the exact kind and quality of behavior that attracts other people's resources: time, help, support, encouragement, money, objects, concern, and honesty. These resources work together with your own efforts to create events and circumstances which lead to enjoyable job conditions in the workplace.

Serving others becomes a permanent talent when you concentrate on removing negative thoughts and commit a portion of your Life Plan goals to improving your performance in the Co-operation Component. Think in terms of serving the needs of others. Whom should you serve? For the Compensation Laws to deliver the best results, you would do well to develop an attitude of service in each and every relationship you encounter. If you become selective or ignore friendly advances of others, you shut off the flow of resources available to you. In business, you must be extremely sensitive to the relationships you have with associates, superiors, and customers as you perform your service.

Service-Minded Attitude

How you view the needs of others who surround you at work will be determined by your mental attitude. You may choose to look at these people as a resource to fill your needs, or as the subject of your criticisms. Or, you may choose to look at these people as an opportunity to demonstrate your ability to share the resources and energy you control. The Law of Recompense states that you will reap what you sow in both kind and quality with exact precision. So, you can sow thoughts of selfishness or thoughts of unselfishness, and reap the rewards of your efforts in accord with the Law.

To serve, by definition, means to help, aid, support, and benefit someone, much like a servant serves his/her master. But this service can either be shared freely with others or be limited by the motivation and attitude of the "server." The "best" service-minded employees recognize that putting the primary emphasis on helping others returns conditions and benefits that are satisfying and rewarding as guaranteed by the Compensation Laws.

Service Jobs

All jobs are designed to contribute meaningful service. Corporate personnel can be classified in three "service" categories. The first is made up of the primary servers: these employees have direct contact with the customer. The next category is comprised of the secondary servers: they serve the customer, but in an unseen role. They assist the primary servers in a manner of which the customer is unaware. The third category is comprised of all other employees.

In a corporation, the primary server may directly provide the customer with the desired product. For instance, the salesperson is a primary associate who turns all of his/her attentions toward the client. This employee interprets, understands, and responds to the needs of the customer. This attentiveness is the mark of a focused organization with a high priority set on serving customers.

The secondary server may type the proposal, process the sales order, assemble the product, or stuff the invoice into an envelope. Responsive, competent personnel are necessary in these jobs to insure that the primary associate's commitment to the customer to deliver a quality product or service is kept in a timely manner.

The third classification, comprised of many support roles, is also extremely necessary in the flow of the business. These people design the product and establish the policies. They include those who supervise or provide the leadership that runs the business. This management group must serve the other two, or the ability to serve the client becomes diminished. In truly successful companies, management actually serves (enables and enhances) the employees of the company, by helping them to be their best.

In all three service categories, it is imperative that service to others be a very top priority. Where are you in this hierarchy? Wherever it is, it is your job to serve customers, or to serve associates who serve customers at one level or another. Your company will benefit from giving good *total*

service, from the first sales call to a possible re-
pair call after delivery. You will benefit by being
associated with a company known in the market
place as a company with outstanding product
quality and customer service.

Understanding Customers

Make an extra effort to know your customer.
The way the customer perceives what you can
provide, and the way you perceive what the
customer wants, can often be miles apart. Understanding its customers' needs makes the difference between the mediocre company and the
great corporation. It is not enough to provide a
good product; your customer must also know that
you provide great total service.

There is a very successful steel-processing
company in my community that makes customer
service a high priority. This company has the philosophy that employees can do better work and
produce products of higher quality if they (the
employees) understand the customer's needs and
problems better. During the course of a year, each
employee is assigned a field trip to visit one of the
company's customers. From welder to department
manager, every employee has an opportunity to
know more about the customers he/she serves.

In your specific job situation you may not have
the same kind of opportunity, but you can learn

about your customers by asking questions and by
listening to your associates who work directly
with them. Typically, this would be marketing,
sales, service, and order-processing personnel,
who have daily contacts and dealings with customers.

Understand that the client does not care about
your company problems. Customers are self-
centered in respect to accomplishing their jobs.
They want to satisfy their own company's needs
or to solve their own company's problems with
your product or service. They are interested only
in receiving their purchases at the agreed-upon
price and on the agreed-upon delivery date. Customers want their needs fulfilled.

Make every effort to follow through with your
job. Finish what you start. Your customer doesn't
care that you're trying hard, if "trying hard" isn't
getting results. Take the necessary steps to provide your customer with what is needed, when it
is needed. Check on deliveries. Make phone calls
to insure promptness. Remind others of their
commitments, and help them if they need assistance. If there are impossible circumstances, find
alternatives, but *serve your customer.*

Loyalty To The Customer

Loyalty to the customer is essential; so keep
your customer's needs and plans to yourself. Just

as you would not discuss any aspect of your own business with your competitors, you must not discuss your customer's business either. Your customer wants and values privacy just as you do; therefore, keep all information confidential.

One of the true tests that determines if a company is going to stay in business is its repeat sales record. Do customers keep coming back and placing more business with your company? Promotional advertising and gimmicks may be successful in enticing a buyer to place the first order, but the quality and performance of the product or service will determine if the customer will buy again or refer others to buy. In any case, the customer who buys and buys again deserves both your company's and your personal loyalty. When the opportunity arises, doing the little extras and extending courtesies will demonstrate your desire to be loyal.

Customer Loyalty

Your customer will return loyalty as long as he/she is provided with quality service. Once your customer knows that you follow through with your commitment to serve, that customer will hold you to your high standards. If service declines or if product quality deteriorates, customer loyalty will disappear. Service and confidentiality must be superior, and they must be maintained at a consistently high level. Everyone in the supplying organization must strive to work together in harmony to provide great total service.

The right mental attitude makes the work easier and the goal of providing great total service achievable. Think about how your job and your performance either directly or indirectly affect a customer's expectations and satisfaction. How competent, committed, and cooperative are you when you perform your duties? Will you handle each task, problem, and assignment with the same intensity and integrity that you would expect if you were the customer? If you find that you may not be performing your best, use QUIET to discover what more you could be doing to help your company maintain its customer loyalty.

The Customer Is Always Right?

When taken literally, the customer's supreme right to be right can be devastating to a business, an organization, or an inexperienced employee. The customer pays the bills and is responsible for the existence of the business, but the customer's being "right" doesn't mean that the business ignores common sense.

The success philosophy that says, "The customer is always right," is simply an attitude regarding the manner in which business affairs relating to the customer's needs are conducted.

The company that makes this philosophy a policy wants the customer to feel that he/she is being treated with respect. For example, a local department store has a "no questions asked" return policy. Store management has taken the position that it is better for their business not to challenge all customers (most of whom are honest) just to catch the occasional culprit who may damage or alter some goods.

When the need does arise to discuss some sensitive issues with a customer, the outcome will likely be successful if a little extra care is given to the communication. Explain the benefits of alternatives, or the practical need to follow through, with both parties working hard to make the original commitment complete. Even bad news can usually be handled by most customers if they have a feeling that they were extended respect, by being notified early and given some options that made sense. In any case, empathy for the customer's view must be paramount in all communications.

Company Spirit

Your company is made up of employees with jobs that are designed to serve customers and make a profit. How well the organization accomplishes these worthwhile goals will depend primarily on the attitude of those employees. Even a few "sour grapes" can adversely affect the performance of the entire organization. If just one person radiates a negative attitude (for example, ignoring a customer or appearing annoyed when interrupted by a customer on the telephone), this negative attitude will likely be felt by the customer, which could easily lead to losing sales.

Some companies have an overall spirit and camaraderie that is positive; they are flowing with underlying energy. There is a sense of teamwork and a high level of excitement. The employees have a great sense of accomplishment, and they achieve their departmental goals.

Other companies appear to be buried in a quagmire, and they perform poorly. These companies are made up of employees who are demoralized. They may lack ambition, and there is little camaraderie. You have, no doubt, heard these remarks: "Who do they think is paying their salaries?"; "You just can't find good help any more!"; "What's wrong with people these days?" These comments are examples from business managers and employees who don't understand that they (business managers and employees) are putting the Law of Attraction to work — in a negative direction.

Most people don't understand what makes the difference between the highly successful company with high-spirited employees, and the mediocre company with employees with poor morale. The cause is not "magic," but in accord with the natural laws of human endeavor. Each employee, including the managers, must have a personal desire to do his/her job to the best of his/her ability. It's a matter of personal attitude — the very thinking of the employee. If the employee thinks a mission is hopeless, he/she will be hopeless. But if the employee thinks that it is possible to accomplish a tough objective, then this employee will act accordingly and help significantly to bring about the desired results.

Management must organize plans, designate priorities, set the tone, and communicate progress, but it can't change the internal motivation of the employee. Each employee must possess, or be willing to develop, a personal desire to succeed. Positive-thinking employees brought together emotionally into a focused activity will accomplish great things. Such an emotional bond among employees produces great success for the company, which in turn flows success back to the employees who made it possible, in accord with the Compensation Laws.

Helping Associates

Help associates with troubling business situations. Of course, you must do your own work, but use some of your "extra" time to help a burdened associate. Offer to assist your supervisor if a project arises for which he/she may require additional support. Make yourself available!

As you help others, they will be attracted by your cooperative attitude, and help will be returned to you in kind and quality. But don't always expect that the people you help will return favors; the return of service may not come from them, but through unexpected channels. However, return to you it will, as promised by the Compensation Laws. Look forward past immediate, tangible results, because you cannot be denied the right to receive the benefits you have conditioned your subconscious mind to work for.

You can plant positive thought seeds in the subconscious of your associates by discussing your ideas, offering suggestions, and stressing the need to think about a given subject. This technique serves equally well for your employees, your peers, and your bosses. One day in passing, I suggested to my boss the need to replace our worn-out office carpet. He didn't seem interested, even before I told him it would cost $30,000! But possibly, he thought afterwards about our professional image or his responsibility to maintain our facilities. In any event, two months later he said to me, "I think you should replace the office carpet." The seed was planted, we got our new office carpet, and my boss was served, too — he was recognized for the office improvement!

You can have a positive influence on associates when you share your service-attitude with them.

Through aiding associates, you will become less critical of their inabilities and less impatient with their mistakes. By viewing your associates as people in various stages of professional growth and personal development, you will come to know that your help and support can influence their thinking and eventually their success as employees.

My new customer service representative quickly developed into a capable employee with the help of my staff members who freely shared their experiences and provided encouragement. Don't limit your involvement to only those employees you may be responsible for. You can have the genuine joy of watching every employee you come into contact with grow and develop into a strong performer for the company. Your reward can be as simple as being a part of a strong company made up of great employees — employees that you have had a hand in developing.

Understand Your Personality

The service-minded attitude may be better understood by using the analogy of two distinct personalities that define the extremes found at the workplace. These extreme examples will help you better understand your own personality, where your personality fits in the work force, and what you need to do to increase the likelihood of

THE INTELLECTUAL CROOK

General Description:

One who mentally uses others, without their knowing, for personal gain.

Typical Characteristics:

- Arrogant
- Blames others
- Dishonest
- Egotistical
- Greedy
- Ignores problems
- Mis-leads
- Misses commitments
- Negative attitude
- Self-centered
- Selfish
- Shallow
- Steals idea
- Stingy
- Vicious

Possible Candidates:

- Associates
- Manager
- Supervisor
- Owner/Corporate

Any employee who demonstrates characteristic behavior.

a more successful career. Both personalities will be discussed in some detail in the following pages.

The first personality defines the "worst case" negative behavior demonstrated by self-centered characteristics. This negative personality is identified as the "Intellectual Crook." The second personality defines the "best case" positive behavior demonstrated by others-directed characteristics. This positive personality is identified as the "Thoughtful Champion." Somewhere in between, you will find yourself. Looking more closely at these service-minded attitudes will help you to understand where you are today, and where you want to be in the future. You can then set into motion the natural laws of human endeavor to improve yourself.

The Intellectual Crook

The Intellectual Crook's behavior is the result of destructive thinking, distorted beliefs, and negative attitudes — activity that has to do with the condition of the mind. This personality's mind is conditioned to "take" as a primary emphasis. Remember, all human endeavors start as ideas or predominant thought in the unseen world of the mind before they are ever manifested in the seen physical world. So, the Intellectual Crook's negative thought (taking) leads to negative actions,

THE THOUGHTFUL CHAMPION

General Description:

One who mentally extends himself/herself for the needs of others without expecting thanks.

Typical Characteristics:

- Attentive
- Considerate
- Courteous
- Discreet
- Fair
- Friendly
- Helpful
- Honest
- Others-directed
- Positive-minded
- Problem Solve
- Respected
- Supportive
- Tactful
- Unselfish

Possible Candidates:

- Associates
- Manager
- Supervisor
- Owner/Corporate

Any employee who demonstrates characteristic behavior.

such as stealing ideas or withholding some information beneficial to an associate.

The Intellectual Crook is motivated by self-interest. The world revolves around him/her, and any relationship, possession, or advantage is fair game. Like everyone, Intellectual Crooks want to receive benefits, feel good, have performance recognized, and achieve success. Unlike everyone, they act like sponges soaking up the resources of others. However, they lose influence as their victims figure out what is happening and move out of their sphere.

When you look at the characteristics of an Intellectual Crook, do you see some elements that are demonstrated by some of your associates, superiors, and customers? Do you see any elements that identify a characteristic you may possess? I think you will agree with me when I say that the Intellectual Crook is a bad guy; but fortunately, there are very few of the really "hard-core" Crooks around.

The Thoughtful Champion

The Thoughtful Champion's behavior is the result of constructive thinking, rational beliefs, and positive attitudes — activity that has to do with the condition of the mind. This personality's mind is conditioned to "give" as a primary emphasis. This behavior is the result of ideas and predominant thought (giving) in which others' needs are in the forefront.

The word "thoughtful" has two connotations that are positive and constructive. The first is that of the "inward" thinking processes, which deal with meditation, visualization, and conceptualizing. To be "thoughtful" is to understand the power of the mind and use this power for constructive purposes. But the second meaning of the word "thoughtful" turns the individual's attention from inward focus to outward focus. To be "thoughtful" is to think and act with the interest of another party. It is a "thoughtful" act to speak to others in a language that they can understand, and act when it can benefit them; to have an attitude that is concerned about the feelings and needs of others while treating them with respect.

This kind and quality of behavior doesn't happen by accident. Humans are born with a self-centered perspective. (The Intellectual Crook is a "child" wearing a business suit.) However, repetitive reinforcement of positive predominant thought evoked by one's environment, or systematic conditioning of the subconscious mind by the conscious mind, can develop a thoughtful personality — the Thoughtful Champion.

The truly thoughtful champions don't need acknowledgment from associates, superiors, and customers. They are willing to extend themselves to help others, because they understand it will always be a growth experience for themselves no matter the outcome. These people know that un-selfish acts are compensated by some channel, as stated by the natural laws of human endeavor.

The Thoughtful Champion is "others-directed." To him/her, the world is a place to create — to create better conditions for others, the business, family, and self. The Thoughtful Champion recognizes that *everyone* wants to receive benefits, feel good, have performance recognized, and achieve success; therefore, they freely supply support and encouragement to others. Thoughtful Champions are well-rounded emotionally, to the point that they have faith and confidence that their efforts to help others will help their business, will serve mankind, and will improve their own station in life as well.

Belief in the working of the natural laws of human endeavor is the basis for this blind faith. Furthermore, ethics, integrity, and honesty are never compromised in any dealings, whether they are with associates, superiors, customers, or suppliers. Every deal is a win-win situation because the Thoughtful Champion will not intentionally withhold any useful information from the other person, even at the risk of losing the deal.

When you look at the characteristics of a Thoughtful Champion, do you see some elements that are demonstrated by some of your associates, superiors, and customers? Do you see any elements that identify a characteristic you may possess? Wouldn't it be great to work for such a

SERVING BEHAVIORAL SPECTRUM

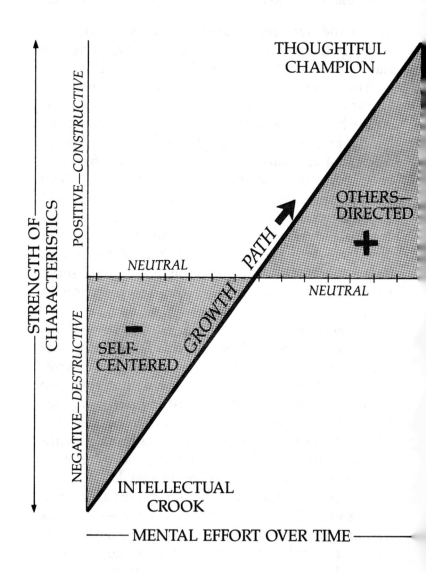

supervisor, or have employees working for you that had all of these positive qualities? Fortunately, there are many employees in American business today who think like the Thoughtful Champion. Remember, all people in business are performing jobs and services consistent with their thinking.

Making Behavioral Changes

Serving associates, superiors, and customers is serious business for the Thoughtful Champion. On the other hand, the Intellectual Crook wants to serve himself/herself. You and I, and most other employees, fit somewhere between these two extreme personalities. It is to your benefit to determine where you are today, and then to set about exchanging negative characteristics for positive characteristics. The Serving Behavioral Spectrum chart indicates that it takes mental effort, expended over time, to move on the growth path toward the more positive characteristics that lead to constructive behavior.

If you are normally a positive thinker about your life and circumstances, you would tend to be located on the Growth Path high on the positive side. Then again, if you are usually positive except for one weakness, such as short temper or impatience, you may be located on the Growth

SERVING CASE STUDY

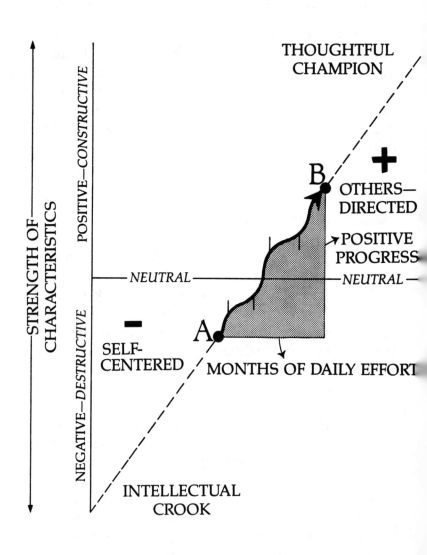

Path a little left of the neutral cross-over point. Although you have many positive attributes, negative mental characteristics pull you down (hold you back). Remember, your position on the Growth Path line is the mathematical sum of the positive and negative qualities of your behavior.

In Chapter 1, I offered the example of my performance on one of my career assignments about which I wasn't excited at first, even though I recognized that I was qualified for the assignment and had the ability to make a contribution. But with mental effort over time I was able to change my attitude, behavior, and, eventually, my performance for the better. The Serving Case Study chart illustrates an approximation of the progress I made in order to replace my self-centered interests and rebellious attitude with positive thoughts of commitment and cooperation.

The actual values of the vertical axis and the horizontal axis are not nearly as important as the relative position of where one is compared to where one needs to be for successful accomplishments. I started at Point A and arrived at Point B in approximately 3 months' time. I had ups and downs along the way and the path wasn't easy, but my daily commitment to my goal of improving my performance was reinforced with the idea that I would continue to learn and develop better business skills if I made my assignment a success; so, I created a goal and achieved!

Serve Unselfishly

It has been said that you can achieve what you desire if you help enough people achieve their desires. You can choose to turn your attention outward to others or inward to serve yourself. It's your choice. If you have the self-motivation to serve others, the natural laws of human endeavor will work for you to bring enjoyable job conditions, career success, and personal happiness. Prepare yourself to receive time, help, encouragement, money, support, objects, concern, and honesty from others as the supply to your demand. *DO* the job by SERVING unselfishly.

Realization

Now you know the "Working for Success" Plan. Both the individual's mental capacity and time are important factors which determine when a desired goal (condition, object, opportunity, performance, problem solution) is achieved. An individual starts this goal-achieving process with an initial mental capacity made up of thinking processes, memory, aptitude, and thinking skill. The daily effort expended to Think, Work, and Serve uses the natural laws of human endeavor to increase this capacity which enhances your ability to perform your job and to accomplish your goals. The "Working for Success" Plan is a "how-to" philosophy you can live by, which will change your business life for the better.

The first key is to THINK constructively. The Creativity Laws, which are the Law of Thought, the Law of Mind and the Law of Cause and Effect, will work for you to create, improve, and develop yourself for success. These natural laws of human endeavor work to start you on the success journey. You have the creative power available within you, and the results of putting it to use are guaranteed by Law. Use QUIET as your success secret!

The second key is to WORK diligently. The Compensation Laws, which are the Law of Recompense and the Law of Attraction, will work for you as you work steadily, earnestly, and energetically. These natural laws of human endeavor work to materialize your desire for pleasant conditions associated with your job. The powerful and silent laws are working tirelessly to bring you the conditions and things you desire. Better job conditions, career opportunities, recognition, and rewards will all come to you as compensation for your physical and mental efforts. Earn your success!

The third key is to SERVE unselfishly. The Growth Laws, which are the Law of Opportunity Supply and the Law of Increase, work for you when you are generous and others-directed. These natural laws of human endeavor work to bring your thoughts of service and success into full maturity. Over time, the outstanding help and support you give to others become the material and energy that sponsor your own growth. Be committed to the thought that associates, superiors, and customers are all very important, and your responsive service will be rewarded. Be a Thoughtful Champion!

The "Working for Success" Plan is a simple program, but it has real power that uses the natural laws of human endeavor to create success for you. Law is no respecter of persons, so use your time wisely and make a strong personal commitment to do the mental work necessary to make the natural laws of human endeavor work for you to achieve success.

Unfortunately, many people give up because they start to believe that their goal is either unrealistic or impossible for them to realize. The important point to remember is that it takes time and effort to achieve both intermediate goals and personal goals. Remember, goals you may set for yourself will either be realistic or only "wishes" in strict accord with your state of professional growth and personal development (mental capacity).

Greater accomplishments leading to greater benefits become possible when using QUIET to concentrate on raising your consciousness. The mental exercise to concentrate on goals and problem solutions will use the natural laws of human endeavor to increase your mental capacity, and by the same method, bring to you greater success. Your success will be the satisfaction of achieving your goals, doing your job to the best of your ability, and knowing you helped associates to be successful at their work.

The mighty and silent natural laws of human endeavor control attitudes and behavior. By working in harmony with these laws, you will be guaranteed success in achieving job satisfaction and career goals. The Creativity Laws take your mental thoughts from small seeds and start the process of bringing your ideas and thoughts into physical reality. Then, the Compensation Laws work to insure that you attract that which you radiate. Your predominant thought and mental images are exchanged for equivalent conditions. And, finally, the Growth Laws work to ripen your goals into the conditions you have consciously cultivated.

To be recognized and compensated as one of the "best" employees, your performance must be viewed by management as worthy of such. You know that the components of Competence, Commitment, and Cooperation contribute directly to your output. You have a formula that leads to establishing a standard or "bench mark" for yourself. You have the knowledge and the power to improve your performance by concentrating on those elements (proficiencies and traits) of the Performance Components that you are not now using positively.

It is not necessary for you to wait for your supervisor to evaluate you, because you can identify where you are weak, and you can discover what you need to do about it. You now know how to think constructively while in QUIET and to give yourself ideas, solutions, and directions. By being honest with yourself and doing the mental work required, you can increase your performance level and be recognized as a very valuable employee.

Helping your associates, supervisors, and customers to solve problems is a worthwhile activity. Every company needs good problem-solvers. You now have special knowledge about the five root problems that cause business concerns and job-related dilemmas. You can recognize the unseen causes of the symptoms that most people believe are the problems. As these problems are caused by people's thoughts, these problems can also be solved by thought. You can use QUIET to find solutions to the complex problems with which you are confronted. You have the power to help your associates and your employer to remove the problems and barriers that hold back the company's growth and success.

Your attitude must be positive if you expect to achieve positive results. Along with high performance level and superior problem-solving skills, your positive attitude rounds out your character and personality. You can learn to ignore the temporary visible effects of circumstances and problems while working to achieve your goals; for it will be your 1-, 3-, 5-, and 10-year goals (or the periods of time you desire) that will lead you to the accomplishment of your major objective. When you spend time in QUIET and learn to see even the smallest progress each day, you will know that you are in control. Successful experiences will become more frequent. In time, you will gain more self-confidence and you will develop a positive attitude as one of your "natural" attributes.

The toughest work you have to do is to learn to depend on your inner self, because you have been trained to always look to someone else. Some expect their employer to provide security, but this dependence on the job should not be one's only means of support. Such a mental attitude makes one unsure and afraid, and fear causes tension and stress. If a person knows that his/her job satisfaction, career success, and personal happiness are his/her responsibility and really depend on his/her state of mind, this person will do better work, be happier, and enjoy life more.

In every condition, you should realize that you have created your own outcome, whether it be success or calamity. You are responsible for your own actions or inactions. The final results are what you, yourself, set out to achieve. You reap what you sow in precise, mathematical balance because the Universe will always be in equilibrium. This phenomenon is also true in the business world. Let these points have time and space in your mind as you work for success:

1. Thinking constructively is a crucial part of performing a job, developing a career, and finding happiness.
2. Before outside sources can be used or blamed for an individual's lot in life or position in business, the individual must first use his/her mental resources to their fullest.
3. Goals are necessary to give life purpose and direction, if the individual's destiny is to have a worthwhile meaning and be a positive contribution to mankind.

4. The mind can be re-directed and conditioned to think about people, events, and circumstances in a positive way.
5. Success habits can be learned; therefore, attitude-habits and resultant behavior-habits can arise from self-talk affirmations.
6. Mental capacity can be developed by daily study, concentration, and exercise; one can achieve one's goals and reach one's potential.
7. No matter the individual's current station in business life, improvements can be made when his/her thinking changes.
8. Better job conditions, greater career success, and finally, personal happiness can be achieved by anyone willing to use his/her mental resources consciously.

Your eventual success depends primarily upon you. You have inherent resources waiting to be used effectively if you choose to do so. Working for your success will take concentrated effort — mental work that impresses new ideas, beliefs, and faith into your subconscious mind. As adults, we tend to stop studying, memorizing, and concentrating on a subject or topic as we did when we were in school preparing for our exams. But by continuing the process many of us have experienced in schools, we will receive life-long benefits when these efforts are directed toward our goals.

NOW, use the Life Plan form in Chapter 7 to record your (1) major objective; (2) intermediate goals; (3) attitude-habits goals; (4) behavior-habits goals; (5) character traits goals; (6) desired bene-

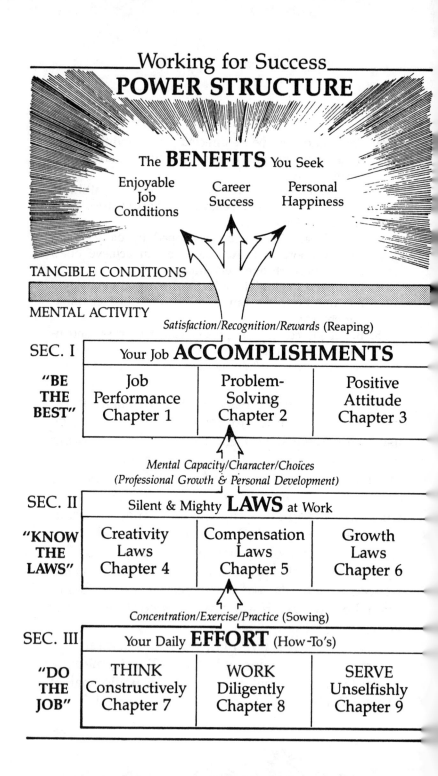

Working for Success
POWER STRUCTURE

The **BENEFITS** You Seek

| Enjoyable Job Conditions | Career Success | Personal Happiness |

TANGIBLE CONDITIONS

MENTAL ACTIVITY

Satisfaction/Recognition/Rewards (Reaping)

SEC. I	Your Job **ACCOMPLISHMENTS**		
"BE THE BEST"	Job Performance Chapter 1	Problem-Solving Chapter 2	Positive Attitude Chapter 3

Mental Capacity/Character/Choices
(Professional Growth & Personal Development)

SEC. II	Silent & Mighty **LAWS** at Work		
"KNOW THE LAWS"	Creativity Laws Chapter 4	Compensation Laws Chapter 5	Growth Laws Chapter 6

Concentration/Exercise/Practice (Sowing)

SEC. III	Your Daily **EFFORT** (How-To's)		
"DO THE JOB"	THINK Constructively Chapter 7	WORK Diligently Chapter 8	SERVE Unselfishly Chapter 9

fits; (7) personal commitment. An organized effort to work in QUIET to discover the right plan for *you*, to concentrate daily upon thinking constructively, working diligently, and serving unselfishly, will produce better job conditions, career success, and personal happiness that flows into other parts of your life.

You have the Power Structure of the "Working for Success" Plan. Take personal control by using this success program consciously. You know how to plant thought seeds of the conditions and things you desire. You know how to work in harmony with the natural laws of human endeavor to increase your performance, which leads to greater accomplishments. You know how to increase your value (product and service) to your employer. Let this knowledge about success principles become part of your consciousness — knowledge transformed into a skill. Under your control, you can transform your daily efforts into enormous successes! In time, you will have the pleasure of witnessing positive improvements in your job, career, character, and personal life.

Every employee in America can enjoy these same benefits by choosing to accept the existence of the natural laws of human endeavor, and by working in harmony with these laws. You have the ability to contribute a valuable service to your associates, superiors, and customers. Use your mental powers to help your employer to be successful, to improve your lot in life, and to give your service and commitment to help America be the best.

ENJOY YOUR JOB. . . . ATTAIN SUCCESS. . . . REACH YOUR POTENTIAL!!!!!

Acknowledgements

Many writers of self-development books have influenced my thinking over the years. One of the most helpful has been Dr. Venice Bloodworth in her book, *Key To Yourself.*

Other authors whose works have helped me gain knowledge and understanding are numerous. I would like to acknowledge those who had the most influence.

U. S. Andersen
Kenneth Blanchard, Ph.D.
Dale Carnegie
Matthew J. Culligan
C. Suzanne Deakins
Jerry Gillies
Shad Helmstetter
Napoleon Hill
Dave Johnson
Charles "T" Jones
Michael LeBoeuf
Richard H. Leftwich
Art Linkletter
Og Mandino

Leon Martel
Joseph Murphy, Ph.D.
John Naisbitt
Norman Vincent Peale
Catherine Ponder
Adele Scheele, Ph.D.
Dr. David Schwartz
Richard S. Sloma
Dennis Waitly
Reni L. Witt
Arthur H. Young
Drea Zigarmi, Ed.D.
Patricia Zigarmi, Ed.D.
Zig Ziglar

NOTES

NOTES

NOTES

NOTES

NOTES

NOTES

LARRY ANDERSON developed the "Working for Success" principles while building a successful career as manager of a multi-million-dollar business. He received his B.S. from Bradley University and his M.B.A. from the University of Dayton. He is a member of National Speakers Association and American Management Association.

With over twenty-five years of industrial business experience, he has provided both technical and management leadership for General Telephone & Electronics Company, Lockheed Missiles and Space Company, McDonnell Douglas Astronautics Company, Industrial Nucleonics Corporation, Reliance Electric Company, Masstron Systems Incorporated, Masstron Scale Incorporated, and Toledo Scale Corporation.

Diagrams and illustrations by Dennis K. Lange
Cover design by Pamela A. O'Rourke

ORDER FORM

Available at your local bookstore, or return this form to:

Anderson & Anderson, Inc.
P.O. Box 26416-A
Columbus, Ohio 43226

Please send me _____ copies of *Working for Success* by Larry Anderson; price $9.95 each.

I understand that I may return any book for a full refund if I am not satisfied.

Name _____

Street _____

City _____ State _____ Zip _____

ORDER SUMMARY

Quantity _____ x $9.95 = $ _____

Sales tax $0.55 per book   + _____
  (Ohio residents only)

Shipping & Handling ($2.50   + _____
  1st book, $1.00 for each
  additional book) Allow 2–4
  weeks.

Total Amount Enclosed $ _____

Make check or money order payable to Anderson & Anderson, Inc.

ORDER FORM

Available at your local bookstore, or return this form to:

Anderson & Anderson, Inc.
P.O. Box 26416-A
Columbus, Ohio 43226

Please send me _____ copies of *Working for Success* by Larry Anderson; price $9.95 each.

I understand that I may return any book for a full refund if I am not satisfied.

Name _____

Street _____

City _____ State _____ Zip _____

ORDER SUMMARY

Quantity _____ x $9.95 = $ _____

Sales tax $0.55 per book   + _____
(Ohio residents only)

Shipping & Handling ($2.50   + _____
1st book, $1.00 for each
additional book) Allow 2–4
weeks.

Total Amount Enclosed $ _____

Make check or money order payable to Anderson & Anderson, Inc.